"A LITTLE COCAINE
TO LOOSEN MY TONGUE"

Sigmund Freud

"A little cocaine to loosen my tongue"

Max Milo

Max Milo éditions, 2023
www.maxmilo.com
ISBN : 978-2-31501-114-8

Freud, a Young Man with Promise

Freud's early work was apparently oriented along three lines.

First, a histological research carried out in the field of animal biology, rather stupefying - it is the case to say it - by its crudity, which will not be erased: the attempt, successful in any case, to locate the sexual organs of the eel, until now hidden from the eyes of science.

Then, an important work on what cannot be said: aphasia, whether it is Wernicke's or Broca's, in its link with lesions of the cerebral cortex.

Finally the enthusiastic discovery of the panacea: the coca leaf, whose chewing cures all the ills and first of all the needs - the hunger that it soothes and the sexual desire, undoubtedly, that it diverts.

These exercises took place against the backdrop of the great discovery of the time, the method of silver staining of tissues by Ramon y Cajal, which reveals the fabulous cellular network that sustains life.

The enthusiastic letters to Martha from this period show a sense of elation, probably as much due to the drug as to the prospect of the fortune that, with fame, awaited the young researcher and would allow the couple to be reunited and established. Sigismund was to be the illustrious son of his own works, and it is remarkable that this self-engendering almost succeeded. But the emphasis put on the analgesic power of the product made him neglect its qualities of local anaesthetic and it was thus the doctor Koller, ophthalmologist to whom he had given the experimentation, who drew a nobelizable glory from it.

In the meantime, in fact, our hero had abandoned his vials to, accepting poverty and hunger, bring his appetites to Martha.

Such a personal experience should have drawn attention to those cases that turn out to be repugnant to addiction and prefer to pay their debt, at least to the god lare (Freud on this occasion already defends his atheism) rather than to the *dealer.*

The nostalgia of what he had thus succeeded/failed will however pursue him in his dreams, without him agreeing to realize that the social environment could only crown the inventor of the panacea, and not the messenger of this common misery that he discovered, which has name *castration* and which reveals itself to be the condition of a later sexual realization.

Freud was nevertheless recognized as the son of his works; but discussed, humiliated, ridiculed, scorned, even by his disciples who were worried that he would not give them a better reputation and that they would be verified as the Jews of the culture.

The unfortunate destiny of the official psychoanalytical movement, which has been struck by intellectual and social conformism since its inception, is probably linked to this original quest for public recognition. To win it, the therapeutic alibi was not far away, but from then on it was obviously quickly overtaken by the drugs - we come back to this - put on the market by the pharmaceutical industry. It is to the point that today research laboratories spend public money to show by statistics the disadvantage of psychoanalytical cures. Besides a very legitimate questioning on the origin of their relentlessness, we will ask the "scientists" who are on the line if it is by behavioral methods that they solve their couple problems, answer their children's difficulties, hold their place as citizens, while keeping a little self-esteem.

But this ultra-rapid course is only worth to remind the permanence in our culture of a death wish, of which the *pharmakon* is the unavoidable representative: delights of the *nepenthe in* order to cure of the life.

Certainly we are on the way to such a path, but it is only accidentally that it comes into our subject. This one has only the ambition to show how his works of young man set up, obviously without his knowledge, the stage on which he was going to discover how the mutilation of his patients was linked to a sexuality forbidden in their words in spite of the immense linguistic network which did not cease articulating it to them.

Charles Melman
September 8, 2005

FROM THE SILENCE OF THE ORGANS TO THE WORD OF THE SUBJECT

The writings of Freud collected in this book have at least a double interest: to inform on the history of practices and ideas at a time, and to give traits, characteristics whose actuality does not let us surprise.

It is essential, if we want to avoid erroneous or even dishonest interpretations, to situate these studies and their writings in their context, their time.

Freud was passionate about science and methodology; he was not yet a great clinician, no doubt because of a lack of practice and patients; he was young and ambitious. He was young and ambitious, both personally and for his practice and its theories. A man of great culture but above all a doctor at that time, he also had the sharp eye of a researcher.

When he is interested in recent works on cocaine, it is not however the eye - and its anesthesia by the future xylocaine - which holds him particularly but, already one could notice, the general energy. Don't the Indians of the Andes, "coca chewers", work without saying a word for hours on end, with so few nutrients other than the magic plant? Don't the soldiers on the battlefields launch themselves into the assaults with an almost inexhaustible energy, which a military doctor will transcribe in his studies?

Freud read these works with avidity and scientific seriousness, but also with the interest of a man who was sometimes subject to headaches, neurasthenia, shyness, fatigue, and various ailments that came to hinder and accompany intense work.

Where does this "extra" delivered by the coca come from? What are the mechanisms of action and the real benefits of this "saving food", saving energy? Where does cocaine intervene to produce its effects?

Thus, mixed with research, another, pragmatic side of Freud's interest is therapeutic use. It is however in these gaps, between exciting research and clinical applications, that the inadequacy will cause the abandonment of cocaine. This aspect is still to be remembered today: fundamental research, clinical experimentation and therapeutic benefits are distinct stages whose conjunction is not given at once. This prudence of interpretation has been somewhat "forgotten" nowadays, when certain so-called fundamental scientific discoveries are considered to be therapeutic progress in a clinic that is always a clinic of the individual.

"Only now do I feel like a doctor," Freud wrote to his fiancée Martha! The magical support for scientific medicine will not be denied, from enthusiasm to abusive prescriptions - issues that are still current. These high hopes were shared in Freud's time, including by a man named Merck, one of the founders of a large pharmaceutical company. The substitution of a product as a means of curing an addiction to a toxic substance is strongly hoped for. Sometimes, often even, with its dramatic aspects: cocaine, to cure alcoholics and morphine addicts, is a dreadful failure.

But Freud's clinical analyses, his own experimentation on himself, described more openly than his dreams, which are more intimate, more revealing but just as much ana-lysed anonymously, interest us because of their relevance. He reports for example this fact: with the cocaine, one feels "normal". What is this normality? That of a body rid of painful sensations; of a mind at work that its exacerbated acuity makes particularly productive, without felt effort. Pushing further than the famous sentence of the surgeon Leriche - "the health is the silence in the organs" -, the catch of cocaine involves moreover a profitability at lower cost. However, the latter is also paid in silence!

Experimentation on oneself was quite common at the time for a doctor. Freud, in addition to the personal benefits that he could temporarily gain from it, mentioned the fact that the variability of the effects observed according to the indi-viduals was thus reduced! When he notes that this variability exists in the same individual, according to the circumstances and perhaps according to the biological dispositions them-selves, it is for him a great disappointment: that of a possible scientific analysis of cocaine. Subjectivity resists there to the universal of science.

But Freud is also and already at Charcot's, where cocaine "loosens his tongue". This master in neurology, a man of the world, studied the pictures presented to him by the hysterical patients: there too, the singularity defied the scientific and

From the silence of the organs to the word of the subject

anatomical rigor of neurology. And it is in the language, in the word and the language that the work will continue!

Jean-Louis Chassaing, psychoanalyst, practicing member of the International Lacanian Association. Former hospital psychiatrist (CHU Clermont-Ferrand).

Letters from Freud to Martha

From *Brautbriefe: Briefe an Martha Bernays aus den Jahren 1882 bis 1886* (Letters to his fiancée, Martha Bernays, years 1882 to 1886), Frankfurt am Main, Fischer Taschenbuch, 1988, pp. 128-143.

Monday 18 January 1886, eleven o'clock in the evening

My sweet little princess,

Yesterday after dinner I worked on my anatomy project until I was exhausted. Today your dear letter finally arrived and I am now obliged to send you this very fragmentary reply, otherwise you will have to wait a long time. I got so tired of writing that I could not hold my pen any longer. The third thing I wanted to tell you about was that I stayed at Charcot's house for over an hour yesterday and he gave me about ten more sheets. I wanted to describe to you what his interior looks like. I'll come back to that later. Also, I'm invited to his house tomorrow night, Tuesday, after dinner, with Ricchetti. "It will be crowded*[1]." You can just about imagine the apprehension mixed with curiosity and satisfaction I feel. Tie and white gloves, even a new shirt, a hairdresser for what's left of my hair, etc. A little cocaine to loosen my tongue. Of course, we can spread the news in Hamburg and Vienna, and even exaggerate, for example with the way he kissed me on the forehead (a la Liszt, etc.). You see, I'm not doing badly, and I'm not making fun of your plans at all.

I kiss you affectionately and I would like to be your dentist, he certainly doesn't know how to appreciate this function at its true value, if not by making you pay the full price.

Your Sigmund

Paris, January 20, 1886

My dear little wife,

...Last night at midnight I wanted to write to you again, but I couldn't find the matches and had to take off my nice suit and go to bed in the moonlight. So let's start at the beginning.

On Saturday, Charcot first approached Ricchetti to invite him to lunch at his home on Tuesday before his departure. He refused, very intimidated, and finally accepted an invitation for the evening after dinner. He then addressed me, repeating the same invitation, and I bowed with deep happiness. He then scheduled our meeting for Sunday at 1:30 p.m. for the translation talks. I have already told you that I went to

---

1. In French in the text. (N.D.T.).

his house and that he gave me ten sheets to start with. I just want to add what his office looks like. It's as big as our future apartment, a room worthy of the fairy castle he lives in. It is divided into two parts, the larger one devoted to science, the smaller one to comfort. They are separated by two slight projections in the wall. As you cross the threshold, you first see the garden through a large three-pane window whose panes alternate with stained glass. Along the two side walls, in the largest part, stands the huge library that occupies two floors. To reach the second floor, one must take the stairs on either side. On the left side of the door, an immensely long table, covered with newspapers and books in a jumble. In front of the large window, on smaller tables, files. Not far from the door on the right is a smaller window, also in multicolored stained glass, and in front of Charcot's desk, all flat, covered with books and manuscripts, his armchair and a host of other seats. In the back, a fireplace, a table and showcases filled with antiques of Hindu and Chinese origin. The walls are covered with tapestries and paintings. Where you can see some of them, they are coated with a Pompeian red. What I briefly glimpsed of the other rooms on Sunday contained the same profusion of paintings, tapestries, carpets and curiosities, in a word, a museum.

After Charcot reminded us of our commitment on Tuesday morning, we had our hands full all afternoon with our preparations. Ricchetti, who was wearing incredibly ragged clothes, had been persuaded by his wife to buy a new pair of pants and a hat. His tailor had probably told him that a suit was not necessary to go to a reception, so he was the only one in a frock coat, without a suit. My own outfit was impeccable, except that I had replaced my unfortunate white system tie with one of my beautiful black Hamburg ties that button up. I had bought a new shirt, a pair of white gloves, the ones I had cleaned having lost their luster, I had had my hair cut and my beard trimmed, which had grown back in the French style, in all, I had spent fourteen francs for this evening. But at least I looked good and made the best impression on myself. We took a car (sharing the expenses). He was terribly nervous, I was quite serene thanks to a small dose of cocaine, although his success was assured, and I had every reason to fear ridicule. We were the first guests and had to wait for these eminent people to leave the table. During this time we examined the magnificent salons. It was then that they arrived and we were in torment. Mr. and Mrs. Charcot, Miss Jeanne Charcot, Mr. Léon Charcot, a young Mr. Daudet, son of Alphonse Daudet, Professor Brouardel, forensic physician, with an energetic and intelligent face, Mr. Strauss, assistant to Pasteur and known for his work on cholera, Professor Lépine of Lyon, one of the most eminent French clinicians, a small, sickly man, M. Gilles de la Tourette, a former assistant of Charcot, now of Brouardel, a true southerner; a Professor Brocke, a member of the Institute, a mathematician and astronomer who immediately began to speak German and turned out to be Norwegian; later Charcot's brother, a gentleman who looked like Professor Vulpian, but it was not him; and a few others whose names I have not learned, as well as an Italian painter, Toffano. And now you are curious to know how I behaved in this distinguished assembly? Quite well. I undertook Lépine whose work I knew, I had long talks with him, then with Strauss and Gilles de la Tourette, I accepted a cup of coffee from Mme Charcot, drank beer later, smoked like a chimney, and I felt very comfortable, without anything bad happening to me. But it was normal to feel at ease, the conversations were not forced, and we were much cared for as strangers. Lépine encouraged me to come to Lyon as well, which I would really like to do, I must have talked a lot about the medical circles in Vienna and I even found myself once in the center of attention. Ricchetti had in fact courted Miss and Mrs. and they came over delighted, announcing "that he speaks all languages*". "And you, Sir*?" asked Mrs. Charcot. I replied, "German, English, a little Spanish and very little French." She thought that was enough and Charcot said, "He is too modest, he only needs to get his ear used*." I then confirmed that I often only understand what I have heard after half a minute and compared this to a pathological symptom of tabes, a remark that was successful.

That was my performance (or rather the performance of the cocaine) and I am very pleased with it. I also got permission to go and listen to Professor Brouardel's lecture in the morgue, which I have already done today. The lecture was very good, but the subject is not very suitable for delicate nerves, and it is being talked about in all the Parisian newspapers as the latest story to make you shudder.

You will perhaps be as interested in the person of Mrs. and Miss Charcot as in my performances. Madame is small, round, lively, with white powdered hair, amiable, of an undistinguished appearance. It is she who is wealthy, her father is said to have countless millions, Charcot was a poor bastard. Miss Jeanne Charcot is very different, also small, a little strong and with a perfectly ridiculous resemblance to her genial father, which makes her so interesting that one does not wonder if she is pretty. She is about twenty years old, very natural and very sociable. I hardly spoke to her, as I stayed with the older gentlemen, but R. talked to her a lot. They say she understands English and German. Imagine that I am not already in love and that I am a real adventurer; I would be strongly tempted to give in to temptation, for there is nothing more dangerous than a young girl who bears the features of a man whom one admires. I would be laughed at, thrown out of the house, and I would have experienced one more beautiful adventure. It's still better this way...

By the way, I am curious to know if this invitation is the last one. I think so, because I owe it to Ricchetti in a way.

(...)

Tender kiss

Your Sigmund

Paris, Tuesday, February 2, 1886

My sweet treasure,

You write so charmingly and sensibly that I feel reassured every time you have given your opinion on something. I don't know how to thank you; I have recently resolved to heed your advice in a particular way; you will laugh; I want to avoid being sick. My fatigue is indeed a kind of benign illness. It's called neurasthenia, and it comes from overwork, worry and restlessness of the last few years, and it has always magically disappeared when I was near you. I must therefore aspire to spend a lot of time with you soon, and this is not possible without our getting married, so I must strive to earn the famous three thousand guilders a year soon; and as I am not lazy and the prospects are not bad, I am not unhappy either and my nervousness does not worry me.

I'm very glad you're giving me credit for thinking of this fee thing. I didn't make a mistake out of thoughtlessness, but out of nobility. There is nothing more to say than what you say, my dear. Indeed, we are young and must learn the hard way. The bookseller has not yet answered my letter. At first I was even embarrassed to tell you about this story, but since it irritated me so much, I couldn't keep it to myself.

Today's news is a kind letter from Obersteiner. As you know, I am hoping for a lot of goodwill from him, even if my intentions are not yet clear. He tells me, for example, what scientific scandals are going on in Vienna. It is good for me to think of this circle of respectable Viennese. One cannot become as bad as people want to say, but one must be careful. The reason for this letter was that he wanted information about the statutes of the Society of Physicians of Paris, which I will be able to get for him this evening. It is indeed six o'clock and at half past nine I am going, as you know, to Charcot's house, not without fearing that I will not have much fun today. The preparations were of course less important today than the first time, but I was so indisposed that I could not work.

The little bit of cocaine I took makes me talkative, my little wife. I keep writing and I accept your criticism of my poor self. Do you know how strange a human being is? His virtues often bear his downfall and his mistakes make his happiness. What you write about the character of the Bernays is quite right. But I have no reason to complain about it. It is to this exaggeration, which you admit so charmingly, that I owe my happiness, I would otherwise never have dared to court you. Are you happy about it too? We won't stop there. But if my life were to come to an end today and I were asked to take stock of it, I would say that in spite of everything - my destitution, the slowness of my successes, the difficulty of getting people's good graces, an exacerbated sensitivity, nervousness and worries - in the simple expectation that you would one day be mine and in the certainty that you loved me, I have been happy. I was always sincere with you, wasn't I? I have never allowed myself, as one usually does with a person of the other sex, to present myself in the best light. I have criticized and berated you relentlessly and in the end I want nothing more than to possess you as you are.

Do you really think I look that nice? I doubt it very much, you see. I think people find me strange, and this is ultimately because in my youth I was not young, and now that I am middle-aged, I cannot manage to grow old. For a long time I have been consumed by my thirst for knowledge and by my ambition, and I have been irritated day after day that nature has not put on my forehead, by a happy caprice, the mark of genius that she sometimes grants. I have known for a long time now that I am not a genius, and I no longer understand how I could even desire to be one. I am not even very gifted, all my abilities to work are probably due to my character and my lack of notable intellectual weaknesses. I know, however, that this mixture is very conducive to slow success, that under favorable conditions I could do better than Nothnagel, to whom I consider myself vastly superior, and that I could perhaps equal Charcot. But I do not say that I shall succeed, for I no longer find these conditions favorable, and I possess neither the genius nor the strength to compel them. But I am so prolix! I wanted to tell you something else. I wanted to explain to you where my inaccessibility and my harshness towards the strangers you mention come from. They are only a consequence of my distrust, after having been often badly treated by common or bad people, and it will diminish as I will have nothing to fear from them, as I will become stronger and more independent. I always console myself by saying that inferior or equal people have never found me unpleasant, it has only ever happened with people who were superior to me in some way. It's hard to guess, but already at school I was ready to oppose with fearlessness as soon as it was a question of defending an extreme position and as a rule to give of myself. When I was for years in a privileged position as the head of the class and was generally trusted, nobody had to complain about me anymore. Do you know what Breuer said to me one night? I was so touched that I later told him the secret of our engagement. He said that he had discovered that behind my apparent shyness lay a being of extreme boldness and daring. I always thought so, without ever having dared to tell anyone. It often seemed to me that I had inherited all the indocility and passion of our ancestors when they defended their temple, as if I were ready to sacrifice my life with joy for a great cause. And at the same time, I have always been so lacking in means, I have never known how to express, even with a word or a poem, the most ardent passions. So I have always repressed my ardor, and that must be felt.

I'm making such a stupid confession to you, darling, and to tell you the truth, there's no reason for it except the cocaine loosens my tongue. But now I want to go down to dinner, then get dressed and write some more. Tomorrow I'll tell you in detail how the evening at Charcot's went. Anyway, you'll say that I had a good time and my letters to Vienna will say the same thing. The truth is for us alone.

Half past midnight

Thank God it's over, and I can tell you right now how right I was. It was boring as hell, only my little dose of cocaine helped. Imagine: there were forty to fifty people there this time and I only knew three or four of them. No introductions were made, everyone did as they pleased. Of course I had nothing to do, I don't think the others had any more fun, but at least they could talk. I spoke even worse than usual. No one cared about me and no one had the time to care. It was normal, I expected it. I bowed to Madame. She apparently wasn't counting on me to entertain her, and she told me that her husband was in the next room. The old man was not very lively, he sat in his chair most of the time and looked very tired to me. Of course he did not fail to enjoin me here and there to take something, that is the only thing I got out of him. Miss was wearing a Greek suit, she was very pretty, I can tell you, your jealousy will not last long, she took my hand at the entrance and did not speak to me all evening. It was only towards the end that I had a political conversation with Gilles de la Tourette during which he prophesied, of course, the most terrible war with Germany. I immediately introduced myself as a Jew, not a German or Austrian. But such conversations are always very painful for me, because I feel something German stirring in me that I decided to suppress long ago. - At about half past eleven, we were invited to go to the dining room where there were many drinks and a snack. I had a cup of chocolate. - Don't think I'm disappointed, you can't expect more than a fixed day* and I only know that we'll manage not to have any. But don't tell anyone how boring it was. We will always talk about the first night.

And now good night, my sweet treasure, I kiss you tenderly.

Your Sigmund

Paris, February 10, 1886

My sweet treasure,

What a charming place Paris is! Shall I tell you about yesterday first or answer all your questions? Yesterday first. It was the most pleasant evening I have ever spent here. I arrived very early and at the same time as Charcot himself, who immediately put me at ease by telling me that I was not his guest, but Mrs. Charcot's. Coming early, however, allowed me to have for myself, first Miss Charcot, then Madame. Mademoiselle was very kind, but, you will be pleased to know, difficult to get to know. I will tell you more later. Madame was soon called back by a whisper from behind, while explaining to me: "It's him, he doesn't know how to tie his own tie*" I was quite happy with this resemblance to the great man. He arrived shortly afterwards and I had him at my disposal for fifteen minutes during which I broached many subjects, first the news of the children's clinic of which he said: "But it's something", then that of my departure, then a small theory that I elaborated on the case that was submitted to me and which pleased him very much, then the translation, etc. He also found that Paris benefited me in many ways. He also found that Paris was taking advantage of me and that "I was getting fat*". The guests arrived little by little and we sat down to dinner. Apart from the Charcot family (four people), there was the sculptor of the statue of Claude Bernard which had just been inaugurated, Richet, Charcot's first assistant with his wife in a very low-cut dress, which one cannot reproach to a very beautiful woman, she was moreover mute as a statue, a Mr. Mendelssohn, a Jew, a doctor, a doctor of medicine, a doctor of medicine, a doctor of medicine, a doctor of medicine, a doctor of medicine. Mendelssohn, a Jew from Warsaw who had been Charcot's assistant and at the same time a pupil of the Berlin physiologists and who worked in very enviable conditions in the Salpêtrière's departments, a M. Arêne, a journalist and art lover, whose articles I read every day in the press, Mr. Toffano, an Italian painter whom I met there for the third time, and myself. I was seated next to Miss Charcot, I send you my place card for our archives. The meal was frugal but composed of choice dishes accompanied by various wines. It was mainly Madame who did the talking, Charcot himself was very cheerful and the family remarked that he was "amiable*". Let us now turn to Mademoiselle. She is twenty years old and very beautiful in spite of her small size, she has of course a lot of confidence in her manners and her interests seem to go mainly towards her father and her brother. "If I were a boy*!" she said, evidently she is very seriously interested in medicine. I tried to be polite and offered to converse in English, but quickly gave up when she began to speak herself and told me that she had learned that language before French. She has a much older sister, but not from the same father; and the remainder of the meal was occupied by a lively discussion between her and young Charcot, which the old man ended by saying in a playful tone, "Enough, Mademoiselle*." After dinner, I had the honor of leading Mademoiselle back to the salon, Mr. Richet being too far away. Having familiarized myself with the place thanks to the dinner, I of course spent a pleasant evening and spoke at length with Charcot himself, who also lent me a book and the issue of a newspaper. During the evening, the appearance of M. Ranvier, the famous historian who had welcomed me so kindly at the Collège de France, was particularly pleasant. I believe that he spoke about me with Charcot and I had then myself a pleasant conversation with him. He did not flatter my qualities as a connoisseur of the human soul when he confessed to me that he would have liked above all to have been a professor in a small German university, such as that of Bonn, for in my letter to Paneth I had defined him as the poor transposition into French of a German academic. The number of guests kept growing, arrived Cornu, the famous ophthalmologist, who really looks great, M. Peyron, director of the Assistance publique against whom the students recently organized a huge heckling, nobody knows why, and - imagine - Daudet himself. A splendid face! Small in stature, he has a narrow head with an incredible mass of black curls, a rather long beard, but not typically French, fine features, great vivacity of movement, a voice that sounds good. Mme Daudet was there too and she stayed all the time next to her husband, she is so ugly that one can't imagine her having been more beautiful one day, lifeless face, protruding cheekbones. She looked like a very young woman, and yet her eighteen year old son who is friends with Charcot's son was there. Daudet is at most forty years old, he must have married very young.

Anyway, the evening was very amusing and I left with Mr. de la Tourette with whom I went to his apartment at 12:30 a.m. to get a job he had promised me.

The next day I couldn't help thinking that I was an ass to leave Paris now that spring is coming and Notre Dame is so beautiful in the sunlight and I would only have to say a word to Charcot to do what I wanted with the patients. But I lack the carefree spirit and courage to prolong my stay.

The next day, that is yesterday, Wednesday, I had another adventure. The Viennese man, an utterly repulsive being, came to get me and we went to the Salpêtrière. The man is a hydrotherapist at Winternitz and therefore thinks he is a great neurologist. He made all sorts of condescending remarks to me, which, aware of a forthcoming revenge, I took lightly. He had a letter of recommendation for Charcot that could not have been more flattering; he had supposedly come to see the greatest living doctor. He was expecting I don't know what kind of reception, but I knew that it would be cold. And in truth, when he handed him the letter, Charcot contented himself with a "At your service, Sir*", adding: "Do you know Mr. Freud*?" Thereupon, disconcerted as he was, and I, with the silent joy I felt, bowed our heads. Then something else happened. There has been a stranger there for a week, a Germanic type, but nevertheless different, whom I could not place. Wednesday is the day we go to ophthalmology, and this stranger suddenly appeared with authority. When he exchanged his card with Charcot's ophthalmologist, the latter became very polite and expressed his hope that Monsieur would come back often so that he could enjoy his presence. We were very curious to find out who he was. Before leaving, he came to us and said: "I heard you speaking German. Let me introduce myself." The other handed him his card first and I was still looking for mine when the stranger said, "I am German, but I emigrated to the United States a long time ago." I finally handed him one of my cards without a title or address. He glanced at it and said, "Are you Dr. Freud from Vienna? I have known him for a long time for his work, especially his work on cocaine. I was a little surprised and asked him his name, which he gave me: "Knapp." Today, Knapp is the leading ophthalmologist in New York, he has also written extensively on cocaine, and I once wrote him a letter from Koller. So I greeted him in the proper way and my Viennese was very surprised, firstly because he did not recognize the man and secondly because, in his haste, he had made a fool of himself once again. When he heard the name cocaine, he asked, "Did you also work on cocaine?" and Knapp replied, "Of course, he led the way." This morning my Viennese was much more fluent and kept talking about the important clientele that awaited me in Vienna.

I got letters again from the bookseller and from Kassowitz. The former is much more polite. Kassowitz writes only to say that he does not want to influence my choice between Breslau and Berlin, he only recommends me, in the latter case, not to say anything about our relations because he is not on good terms with the Berlin doctors. I am very busy working on the case that Charcot has entrusted to me. Our relations continue to be very satisfactory.

But now it's time to answer your questions. I don't know anything about the company's funds, I think it's private like other polyclinics, and it probably has to operate on voluntary contributions. There is no question of paying a department head, which is not at all detrimental to his situation. The consultation takes place in a room set aside for this purpose, in which there is also an electrical device. One or two students serve as assistants in keeping the books. The consultation takes place two or three times a week, it is free of charge, you can get documentation and when you are a teacher you can develop courses from this documentation, if not for now, at least for the winter. Do you understand now? It is this documentation that is the main advantage, as well as the renown that one obtains in one's specialty. - I never told you anything about the uncle in Breslau because I never think about him. I have seen him three times in my life, for a quarter of an hour each time. He is a younger brother of my father, a rather common person, he is a merchant and his family is very sad. Among his four children, the only healthy one is a girl married in Poland. One of his sons is what is called hydrocephalic and feeble-minded, another who seemed promising when he was young, became insane at nineteen, as well as a twenty-one year old girl. I had been so good at hiding this character that I had always imagined that my family had no neurological disorders. But since I think about Breslau, the fact that one of the sons of my other - very unhappy - uncle in Vienna died of epilepsy has come back to me. I can no longer blame his mother's family for this heredity, and I am forced to admit to myself that I have a neuro-pathological defect, as they say. Fortunately, there is little to report among us seven siblings, except that - apart from Emmanuel - Rosa and I have a very nice tendency to neurasthenia. As a neurologist myself, I fear these stories almost as much as a sailor fears the sea. But you, my dear, see that you must remain in good nervous health if you want the three children of whom you already dream so boldly to be healthy. And if medicine scares you, my darling, I can't blame you at all, but you must love me, and if we marry soon, we will be very happy all the same. These stories are so common in Jewish families. But I have talked enough about medicine.

I kiss you tenderly, my little wife. I finish another day than the one I started and tomorrow I expect a new letter from you.

Your Sigmund

ABOUT COCA

First published in 1884 in *Centralblatt für die gesammte Therapie (Central Journal for Comprehensive Therapy)*, vol. 2, July, pp. 289-314. Freud wrote this study after indulging for two months in cocaine. In response to demand, he had it reprinted with four additional remarks. The booklet appeared in 1885.

I. The plant

Coca, *erythroxylon coca*, is a 4 to 6 foot tall shrub similar to our thorny plum tree, which is grown in large quantities in South America, particularly in Peru and Bolivia. Its favorite places are the warm valleys of the eastern slopes of the Andes, 5,000 to 6,000 feet above sea level, in a very humid climate and free of extreme temperatures[2]. The leaves that serve as an indispensable consumer product[3] to some 10 million human

---

2. O. R. Markham, *Peruvian Barks*, London, 1880.
3. From an estimate by Bibra: *Die narkotischen Genußmittel (The narcotic consumer products)*, 1855.

beings are "oval, 5 to 6 cm long, petiolated, with full-edged, plumose leaves, characterized by two particularly prominent linear folds on the lower part that, like lateral veins, accompany the median vein from the base of the leaf to its apex, in the shape of a low arch[4]". The small white flowers of the shrub are presented by 2 or 3 in side tufts and the fruits are red and oval. It is planted either from seed or cuttings; the young plants are transplanted after a year and give their first crop of leaves after 18 months. The leaves are considered mature when they have become so rigid that touching them causes the stems to break.

They are then quickly dried in the sun or fire and sewn into bags (*cestos*) for transport. A coca bush cultivated in optimal conditions gives 4 to 5 harvests of leaves per year and remains productive for 30 to 40 years. In these countries, when production is good (reportedly 30 million pounds per year), coca leaves are an important commercial commodity and generate significant taxes[5].

II. History and use of the site

When the Spanish conquerors arrived in Peru, they discovered coca, which was cultivated there and enjoyed great prestige, to the point of being intimately linked to the religious customs of the population. The legend tells that in immemorial times, Manco Capac, the divine son of the sun, came down from the cliffs of the lake Titicaca and brought the light of his father

---

4. I owe this description to Professor Vogl in Vienna who kindly made his notes and books on coca available to me.
5. Weddell, *Journey in the north of Bolivia*, 1853.

to the miserable inhabitants, that he taught them to know the gods, to exercise the utilitarian arts, and that he offered them the coca, this divine plant that satiates the hungry, strengthens the weak and makes them forget their bad fortune[6]. The leaves of coca were offered in sacrifice to the gods, one chewed some while celebrating the services, one put some even in the mouth of the dead to assure them a favorable reception in the beyond. As a chronicler of the Spanish conquest reports[7], himself descendant of the Incas, the coca was at first a rare commodity in the country, its consumption was then a privilege of the sovereigns; at the time of the conquest, it had however become accessible for a long time to everyone. Garcilasso tried to protect coca from the anathema of the conquistadors. The Spaniards did not believe in the miraculous effects of this plant which was suspected to them, as a work of the devil, because of its role in the religious ceremonial of the defeated. A Council of Lima even forbade its consumption, which was considered a pagan and sinful practice. But their attitude changed when they noticed that the Indians could not carry out the difficult work which one imposed to them in the mines if one deprived them of coca. They deigned to distribute coca leaves 3 or 4 times a day to the workers and to grant them short breaks to chew the precious leaves, and so coca has been maintained among the natives until today; there are even traces of the religious cult of which it was the object[8].

---

6. Scrivener, "On the coca leaf and its uses in diet and medicine," *Medical Times and Gazette*, 1871.
7. Garcilasso de la Vega, *Comentariós reales de los Incas*, 1609-1617.
8. Christison, "Observations on the effect of cuca, or coca, the leaves of Erythroxylon Coca," *British Medical Journal*, 1876.

The Indian always carries a bag of coca leaves (called *chupsa*) on his excursions, as well as a bottle of the plant's ashes (*llicta*)[9]. In his mouth, he forms a ball from the leaves (*acullico*), pierces it several times with a point immersed in the ash[10] and chews it slowly while salivating profusely. In other regions, a kind of earth, *tonra*, is added to the leaves instead of the ash[11]. Chewing three to four ounces of leaves daily is not considered excessive. According to Mantegazza, the Indian starts consuming this product at a very young age and continues until the end of his life. When he has to travel a difficult path, when he takes a wife, and in general when his forces are particularly solicited, he increases the usual dose.

(The reasons for adding the alkalis present in the ash are not clear. Mantegazza reports that he chewed coca leaves with and without *llicta* and felt no difference. According to Martius[12] and Demarle[13], the alkalis in the plant's ash release cocaine probably associated with tannic acid. The *llicta* analyzed by Bibra was composed of 29% calcium carbonate and magnesia, 34% potassium salts, 3% iron aluminate, 17% insoluble combinations of alumina, iron silicate, 5% carbon and 10% water).

There is a profusion of testimonies about the unusual fatigue that the Indians endure under the effect of coca and the hard work that they accomplish without needing to really eat[14].

---

9. Mantegazza, *Sulle virtù igieniche e medicinali della coca*, Milano, 1859.
10. Scrivener, *loc. cit.*
11. According to Ulloa.
12. *Systema mat. med. brasil*, 1843.
13. *Essay on the coca of Peru*, thesis, Paris, 1862.
14. See Fronmüller, "Coca und Cat.", *Prager Vierteljahrsschrift für praktische Heilkunde (Prague Quarterly Journal of Practical Medicine)*, vol. 79, 1863.

Valdez y Palacios[15] indicates that the Indians walk hundreds of hours at a faster pace than horses, without showing signs of fatigue. Castelnau[16], Martius[17], Scrivener[18] confirm it and Humboldt speaks about it as an established fact in relation to his journey in the equinoctial regions. It is quoted a lot what Tschudi[19] reports of the works carried out by a *cholo* (mestizo) that he could observe with precision. This one executed for him painful works of exhumation during five days and five nights without sleeping more than two hours per night and without absorbing something else that coca. Once the work was done, he accompanied him in a ride that lasted two days, running beside his mule. He said that he would be willing to do the same work again without eating if he was given enough coca. This man was 62 years old and had never been sick.

The Voyage of the Novara frigate tells similar examples of forces multiplied by the coca. Weddell[20], von Meyen[21], Markham[22], even Poeppig[23] who has widely decried it, can only confirm these effects of coca which have not ceased to amaze the world since they have been known.

Other reports emphasize the ability of *coqueros* (coca chewers) to withstand prolonged starvation without

---

15. *Viagem da cidade de Cuzco a de Belem*, 1840.
16. *Expedition to the central parts of South America*, 1851.
17. Spix and Martius, *Reise in Brasilien (Journey to Brazil)*, 1831.
18. *Loc. cit.*
19. *Reiseskizzen aus Peru in den Jahren 1838 und 1842 (Notes from a trip to Peru in the years 1838 and 1842)*.
20. *Loc. cit.*
21. *Reise um die Welt (Journey around the world)*, 1835.
22. *Travels in Peru and India*, 1862.
23. *Reise in Chili, Peru und auf dem Amazonenstrom (Journey to Chile, Peru and the Amazon River)*, 1827-1832.

About coca

complaint. According to Unanuè[24], only the inhabitants who consumed coca were able to survive the famine that occurred in 1781 in the besieged city of La Paz. According to Stewenson, people in many areas of Peru often abstained from food for several days because of coca without interrupting their work.

Given all this evidence and the role that coca has played in South America for centuries, we can reject the view that the effect of coca is sometimes imaginary and that the natives are also able to achieve the performances cited without it, because of the strain inherent in their situation and their training. One would expect to hear, however, that the *coqueros* compensate with an increased intake of food at times of rest or that their lifestyle leads them to rapid degeneration. The first point can certainly not be deduced from the travelers' reports; as for the second, reliable witnesses have decisively contradicted it. Poeppig has certainly sketched a frightening picture of the physical and intellectual decay that regular consumption of coca is supposed to have as an inescapable consequence, but all other observers are of the opinion that moderate consumption of coca is more beneficial than harmful to health, and that the *coqueros* reach a venerable age[25]. However, according to Weddell and Mantegazza also, the immoderate consumption of coca generates a cachexia which is expressed physically by difficult digestion, emaciation and other related phenomena, mentally by an ethical depravity and a perfect apathy, except in the consumption of the exciting product. Whites have sometimes succumbed to this condition which has many

---

24. *Disertacion sobre el aspecto, cultivo, comercio y virtudes de la famosa planta del Peru nombrada Coca*, Lima, 1794.
25. Fronmüller, *loc. cit.*

similarities with chronic alcoholism and morphinism. It should be noted that cachexia is always attributed to the toxic effect of coca in case of immoderate consumption, and never to any disproportion between the absorption of food and the work performance of the *coqueros.*

III. Coca leaves in Europe - cocaine

According to Dowdeswell[26], the oldest recommendation of the coca is found in a writing of the doctor Monardes (Seville, 1559) which appeared in an English translation in 1596. As the later communications of the Jesuit Padre Antonio Julian[27] and of the doctor Pedro Crespo[28], both in Lima, it praises the extraordinary virtues of the plant against the hunger and the fatigue. These two authors put a lot of hope in the introduction of the coca in Europe. The plant was brought to Europe in 1749, described by A. L. de Jussieu and classified in the genus *erythroxylon,* then introduced by Lamarck as *erythroxylon coca* in his *Encyclopédie méthodique botanique* in 1786. The reports of travelers like Tschudi, Markham, etc., brought the proof that the action of the coca leaves is not limited to the Indians.

Paolo Mantegazza, who lived many years in the South American coca countries, published his experiments on the physiological and therapeutic effects of coca leaves in both

26. *The Coca Leaf,* Lancet, 1876.
27. *Disertacion sobre Hayo ó Coca,* Lima, 1787.
28. *Memoria sobre la coca,* Lima, 1793.

hemispheres in 1859[29]. Mantegazza is an enthusiastic panegyrist of coca, he provided evidence of its multiple therapeutic possibilities by presenting cases of patients. His publication attracted attention, but did not inspire great confidence. I have encountered so many correct remarks in Mantegazza that I am inclined to give value even to indications that I have not had the opportunity to verify.

In 1859, Dr. Scherzer brought back coca leaves from the expedition of the Austrian frigate *Novara* to Vienna. He sent some of them to Professor Wöhler for analysis. From these leaves, a student of Wöhler's, Niemann[30], prepared an alkaloid, cocaine; after Niemann's death, another student of Wöhler's, Lossen[31], continued the research on the substances contained in coca leaves. Cocaine (Niemann's) crystallizes according to the large, colorless, 4-6-sided prisms of the clinorhombic system. Its taste is bitter and causes an anaesthesia of the mucous membranes. It melts at 98°, is hardly soluble in water[32], easily soluble in alcohol and ether and in diluted acids. It gives double salts with platinum and gold chloride. On heating with hydrochloric acid, it decomposes into benzoic acid, methylene alcohol, and a little-studied base, *ecgonin*. Lossen established the formula of cocaine: $C17H24N4$. Because they are highly

---

29. *Sulle virtù igieniche e medicinali della coca*, dissertation awarded the Dell Acqua prize in the 1858 competition, from *Annali Universali di Medicina*, 1859. - A brief review of this work can be found in the *Österreichischen Zeitschrift für praktische Heilkunde (Austrian Journal of Practical Medicine)* of the same year.
30. *Annalen der Chemie und Pharmacie*, 114.
31. *Ibid*, 133.
32. Regarding the solubility of cocaine in water, the author's indications are not very concordant. Several preparations have obviously been marketed and used as "cocaine".

soluble in water, salts of hydrochloric acid and acetic acid are particularly suitable for physiological and therapeutic use[33].

In addition to cocaine, the following have been found in coca leaves: the tannic acid of coca, a characteristic wax and a volatile base, hygrin, whose odor is reminiscent of thrimethylamine and which Lossen obtained in the form of a viscous, light yellow oil. According to some indications contained in the communications of the chemists, the series of new substances which compose the coca leaves does not seem to be exhausted yet.

Since the discovery of cocaine, many observers have studied the action of coca on sick and healthy animals and humans. For this purpose, they have used a preparation called cocaine, infused coca leaves or prepared in the Indian way. In Austria, it was Schroff senior who made the first experiments on animals in 1862; there are other communications on coca by Frankl (1860), Fronmüller (1863) and Neudörfer (1870). In Germany, the therapeutic recommendation of Clemens (1867), the animal experiments of von Anrep (1880) and the experiments of Aschenbrandt on exhausted soldiers (1883) should be mentioned.

In England it was A. Bennett made the first experiments on animals in 1874; the communications of the very old president of the British Medical Association, Sir Robert Christison, were much noticed in 1876; and when a correspondent of the *British Medical Journal* affirmed that Mr. Weston, whose walking performance astounded the whole scientific world

---

33. Husemann and Hilger, *Die Pflanzenstoffe... (The Substances of the Plant...)*, 1884.

of London, chewed coca leaves, coca became for a time the object of general interest. The same year (1876), Dowdeswell published an experimental study carried out in the physiological laboratory of the University College without any result; since then, the coca seems not to have been any more the object of any experiment in England[34].

As far as French publications are concerned, we should mention: Rossier (1861), Demarle (1862), Gosse's monograph on *Erythroxylon Coca* (1862), Reiss (1866), Lippmann, (*Étude sur la coca du Pérou*, 1868), Moréno y Maïz (1868) who gave a new preparation of cocaine, Gazeau (1870), Collin (1877), and Marvaud in *Les Aliments d'épargne* (1874), the only one I had at my disposal among the documents mentioned.

In Russia, Nikolsky, Danini (1873), Tachanoff (1872) have particularly studied the effects of cocaine on animals; from North America have arrived in recent years many reports on the successful therapeutic use of coca preparations, an account of which was made in the *Detroit Therapeutic Gazette*.

Among the quoted works, the oldest ones had as a whole the consequence of arousing a great disappointment and the conviction that one could not hope to find in Europe the effects of coca which had been praised in South America. Research like that of Schroff, Fronmüller, Dowdeswell gave negative results or at least not very significant. There is more

---

34. To gather all the material, I used the article "Erythroxylon Coca" in the index of the *Catalogue of the Library of the Surgeon-General's office*, vol. IV, 1883, which can almost be considered a complete bibliography. Because of the inadequacy of our public library, I have had to make do with citations and references for some of the cited material on coca, but I hope I have read enough to satisfy the purpose of this presentation: to establish the value of coca.

than one explanation for these failures. The quality of the preparations used is the main reason[35]. Many authors even express their doubts about the quality of their preparations, and insofar as they still give credence to travelers' reports on the effects of coca, they assume that these must be attributed to a volatile component of the leaf. For this, they rely among other things on the statements of Poeppig, who indicates that in South America, it was considered that even leaves that had been kept too long were no longer worth anything. However, recent experiments with cocaine prepared by Merck in Darmstadt have shown that the effects of coca in Europe and South America are due to cocaine and can be used for dietary and therapeutic purposes.

IV. The effect of coca in animals

Since we know that animals of different species - as well as individuals of the same species - never differ more from each other than in those chemical peculiarities which condition their sensitivity to substances foreign to their organism, we will not expect a priori to find in animals effects of coca leaves analogous to the effects described on human beings. It will be considered as a satisfactory result to be able to apprehend these two kinds of effects by adopting homogeneous points of view.

---

35. The cocaine content of coca leaves fluctuates according to Lossen between 0.2% and 0.02%. 0.05 g of *cocainum muriaticum* seems to be the effective dose for humans. According to Lippmann (*Étude sur la coca du Pérou*, thesis, Strasbourg, 1868), a dried coca leaf weighs one decigram.

It is to von Anrep[36] that we owe the most thorough experiments concerning the effects of coca on animals. Before him, such experiments had been made by Schroff father[37], Moréno y Maïz[38], Tarchanoff[39], Nikolsky[40], Danini[41], Al. Bennett[42] and Ott[43]. Most of these authors employed the alkaloid orally or by subcutaneous injection.

The most general result of these researches is that cocaine has, on the nervous system, an exciting action in small doses, a paralyzing action in high doses. The paralyzing action is particularly significant during the poisoning of cold-blooded animals, while in warm-blooded animals, it is the manifestations of excitation that predominate.

According to Schroff, cocaine generates a soporific state in frogs with paralysis of voluntary muscles. Moreno y Maïz, Danini, Nikolsky and Ott obtained essentially the same results; Moreno y Maïz indicates that in case of small doses, tetany precedes general paralysis; under the same conditions, Nikolsky describes a stage of excitation of the musculature, Danini on the other hand has never observed spasms.

---

36. *"Über* die physiologische Wirkung des Cocains" (On the physiological effects of cocaine), *Pflügers Archiv*, XXI, 1880.
37. "Vorläufige Mitteilung über Cocain" (Provisional communication on cocaine), *Wochenblatt der Gesellschaft der Ärzte in Wien*, 1862.
38. *Chemical and physiological researches on erythroxylon coca from Peru*, 1868.
39. *Cocain und Diabetes*, 1872 (in Russian).
40. *Beitrag zur Cocainwirkung auf den Tierorganismus (Note on the effects of cocaine on the animal organism)* (in Russian).
41. *Über physiol. Wirkung und therap. Anwendung des Cocains (The physiological effect and therapeutic use of cocaine)*, 1872 (in Russian).
42. "An experimental inquiry into the physiological action of Theine...", *Edinburgh Medical and Surgical Journal*, 1874.
43. Coca and its alkaloid cocain,. *New York Medical Record*, 1876.

Also according to von Anrep, cocaine has a paralyzing effect on frogs after a brief moment of excitement; the sensitive nerve endings are indeed impeded, then the sensitive nerves themselves. At first, breathing speeds up, then calms down, the heartbeat slows down to a diastolic stop. Doses of 2 mg are enough to cause symptoms of intoxication.

According to Schroff's experiments on rabbits, which are not very consistent in detail, cocaine causes various spasms, an increase in the frequency of breathing and pulse, dilation of the pupils and, with further spasms, death. The outcome of the intoxication is strongly dependent on the mode of application. According to Danini, cocaine intoxication in homeotherms first causes excitement expressed by continuous jumping and running, then muscle paralysis, and finally clonic cramps. In dogs, after administration of coca, Tarchanoff found an increase in the secretion of mucus and sugar in the urine.

According to von Anrep's experiments, the effect of cocaine on homeotherms initially consisted, even at high doses, of a lively excitation of the psyche and of the brain centers controlling voluntary movement. With a dose of cocaine of 0.01 g per kilo, the dogs show clear signs of joyful excitement and a manic need to move. Von Anrep sees these movements as a sign that all the nerve centers are affected by the excitement, and he also analyzes certain pendular movements of the head as symptoms of a stimulation coming from the semicircular canals. To the picture of the second state that cocaine provokes belong in addition: the increase of the respiratory frequency, a strong acceleration of the pulse due to a very fast paralysis of the vagus nerve, a dilatation of the pupils, an acceleration of the intestinal movements, an important increase of the blood pressure and a decrease of the secretions. At high doses, striated muscles also remain intact, high doses that eventually cause spasms, signs of paralysis and death by paralysis of the respiratory system. For dogs, von Anrep did not determine the lethal dose; for rabbits it is 0.10 g and for cats 0.02 g per kg[44].

If the spinal cord is separated from the bulb, cocaine no longer causes spasms or increases in blood pressure (Danini); if the dorsal medulla is transected, spasms occur in the front legs, but not in the hind legs (von Anrep). Danini and von Anrep assume for this reason that the action of cocaine is mainly confined to the vital area of the bulb.

It should also be mentioned that only Schroff Sr. considers cocaine as a narcotic and puts it on the same level as opium and cannabis, while almost all the others put it with caffeine.

V. The action of cocaine on healthy human beings

Through repeated experiments on myself and others, I studied the effects caused by the absorption of cocaine on a healthy organism, and I found them to be essentially consistent with the effects of coca leaves described by Mantegazza[45].

The first time, I took 0.05 g of *cocainum muriaticum* in a 1% water solution, when I was in a dull mood due to fatigue.

---

44. In subcutaneous injection.
45. Like Aschenbrandt (*Deutsche medicin. Wochenschrift*, Dec. 1883), I used the chloride cocaine prepared by Merck in Darmstadt. The same can be obtained in Haubner's pharmacy "Engelapotheke am Hof" at a price not much higher than Merck's, but still very high. According to what I was kindly told, the management of this pharmacy is trying to lower the prices by contacting other sources of supply.

This solution is relatively viscous, slightly opalescent, with a strange aroma. Its initially bitter taste turns into a series of very pleasant aromas. The dry salt of cocaine has the same smell and the same taste in more pronounced.

A few minutes after drinking, one has a sudden feeling of cheerfulness, then of lightness. At the same time, lips and palate become pasty, then one has a sensation of warmth in the same places, and if one drinks cold water, it seems warm on the lips, cold in the throat. At other times, a pleasant sensation of freshness in the mouth and throat prevails.

During this first experience, I noticed a brief toxic effect that I did not regain afterwards. I began to breathe more slowly and deeply, felt exhausted and drowsy, frequently needed to yawn, and was quite pleased with myself. After a few minutes, the euphoria associated with cocaine began, accompanied by many refreshing flashbacks. Immediately after taking cocaine, I noticed a slight slowing of my pulse and then a moderate acceleration.

I observed the same physical symptoms in others, mostly of the same age. Repeated refreshing dismissals have proven to be the biggest constant. At the same time, gurgling sounds are often heard that must come from the upper intestines. Two of the people I had observed claimed to be able to recognize the movements of their stomachs and assured me that they had felt them on several occasions. I was frequently told of an intense sensation of heat in the head at the beginning, a sensation which I myself experienced in later experiments and which I did not find again on other occasions. Cocaine caused dizziness in only two cases. On the whole, the toxic symptoms due to the absorption of cocaine are short-lived, less intense than those caused by powerful doses of quinine or sodium salicylate, and they seem to diminish further with repeated consumption.

The occasional effects added by Mantegazza are: transient erythema, increased urine output, dryness of the conjunctiva and nasal mucosa. Dryness of the mucosa of the mouth and throat is a constant and a symptom lasting several hours. Some observers (Marvaud, Collan) have indicated slightly laxative effects. Urine and faeces apparently take on the smell of coca. The action on the frequency of the pulse is very variously described by the various observers. According to Mantegazza, coca causes a rapidly significant increase in pulse rate; at higher doses, it increases further. Collin[46] also observed an acceleration of the pulse, while Rossier[47], Demarle[48] and Marvaud observed that the acceleration of the beginning was followed by a more durable slowing down. Christison noticed on himself that by consuming coca, a body work caused an acceleration of the pulse weaker than usual. Reiss denies any influence on pulse rate. I have no difficulty in explaining this lack of homogeneity, firstly by the diversity of the preparations used (a hotter infusion of the leaves, a cold cocaine solution, etc.) and of the applications[49], secondly by the diversity of individual reactions. With coca, the latter is to be taken into account in a very pronounced way, as Mantegazza has already said. There are probably people who cannot tolerate coca at all, and I have also met a considerable number of people for

---

46. "Of coca and its true therapeutic properties" *L'Union médicale*, 1877.
47. "On the physiological action of coca leaves," *Swiss Medical Echo*, 1861.
48. *Essay on the coca of Peru*, thesis, Paris, 1862.
49. See the results of the subcutaneous injections above.

whom the 5 cg dose, which is effective for me and for others, has no effect.

Psychically, *cocain. muriat.* in doses of 0.05 to 0.10 g causes a cheerfulness and a lasting euphoria, which do not differ at all from the normal euphoria of a healthy man. The sense of impairment that accompanies alcohol-induced mirth is totally absent, as is the need for immediate activity characteristic of the effects of alcohol. One feels more self-control, more alert and more able to work; but in working, one does not feel that precious excitement and increase of intellectual capacity caused by alcohol, tea or coffee. You feel as if you are in a normal state, and you soon find it hard to believe that you are under the influence of any drug[50].

It is as if the mood induced by cocaine in such doses is not so much caused by direct excitement as by the suppression, in a general state of mind, of depressing elements. It may be safe to assume that the euphoria of a healthy person is nothing more than the normal mood of a well-fed cerebral cortex that "knows nothing" about the organs of his body.

During this state linked to cocaine and whose definition remains approximate, intervenes what one considered as the wonderfully stimulating effect of the coca. A work of long duration, of a great intellectual or muscular intensity, is carried out without tiredness, and one does not feel any more the need to eat or sleep which generally arises in an imperative way at certain hours of the day. With cocaine, one can eat copiously and without disgust when invited to do so, but one clearly has

---

50. It is Wilder's account (*Detroit Therapeutic Gazette*, Nov. 1882) that best accords with my own observations.

the feeling of not having needed that meal. Similarly, in the waning phase of the effects of cocaine, one may fall asleep when going to bed, but one may also go without sleep without any difficulty. During the first few hours, sleep is not possible, but this insomnia is not painful.

I have tested on myself about a dozen times that coca protects against hunger, sleep and fatigue and stimulates mental work; I have not had the same experience with physical work.

I was able to observe a very good example of suppression of extreme fatigue and a very justified feeling of hunger in a colleague who, fasting since the morning, took 0.05 g of *cocain muriat.* at 6 pm after a tiring activity. A few minutes later, he said he felt like leaving the table, did not want to have dinner and felt ready for a long walk.

This stimulating effect of the coca has been attested in an unmistakable way by a series of reliable communications, including in the last years.

At the age of 78, Sir Robert Christison[51] inflicted on himself, for the purposes of the experiment, fatigue to the point of exhaustion by walking 15 English miles without taking any food. He did it again a few days later with the same result; during the third experiment, he chewed 2 drachmas of coca leaves, walked the same way there and back without any pain, felt, once back home, in spite of an abstinence having lasted 9 hours, neither hungry nor thirsty, and woke up the next morning without feeling tired. Another time he climbed a 3,000 foot mountain and reached the top totally exhausted.

---

51. "Observations on the effect of cuca, or coca...", *British Medical Journal*, 1876.

Under the effect of coca, he made the descent with a youthful spirit and without any fatigue.

Clemens[52] and J. Collan[53] found similar effects on themselves, the latter during hikes of several hours on snow. Mason[54] says of coca that it is "an excellent thing [...] for a long walk" and Aschenbrandt[55] recently reported that Bavarian soldiers who had been exhausted by fatigue and illnesses that had weakened them were able, after an administration of coca, to participate in exercises and marches. Moreno y Maïz[56] was able to stay up all night long consuming coca. Mantegazza remained without eating for 40 hours under the effect of coca. We are therefore allowed to assume that the effect of cocaine on Europeans is the same as that of coca leaves on South American Indians.

The effects of a moderate dose of cocaine decline so gradually that it is difficult to determine their duration under normal conditions. When one works intensely on cocaine, the feeling of well-being diminishes after 3 to 5 hours and one needs another dose of coca to avoid fatigue. When one does not perform any hard muscular work, the effect of coca

---

52. "Erfahrungen über die therap. Verwendung der Cocablätter" (Experiments on the therapeutic use of coca leaves), *Deutsche Klinik*, 1867.
53. J. Collan, *Finska läkaresällsk*, XX, 1878, after Schmidt's Jahrbüchern, 87, 1880.
54. "Erythroxylon coca; its physiological effects...", *Boston Medical and Surgical Journal*, 1882.
55. "Die physiologische Wirkung und Bedeutung des cocain. muriat. auf den menschlichen Organismus. Beobachtungen während der Herbstübungen des Jahres 1883 beim III. Bayerischen Armee-Corps" (The physiological effects and importance of *cocain. muriat.* on the human organism. Observations made during the autumn 1883 maneuvers on the 3rd Bavarian Army Corps), *Deutsche medicinische Wochenschrift*, December 12, 1883.
56. *Loc. cit.*

seems to last longer. It is said in a quite concordant way that to the euphoria felt under coca does not succeed any state of lassitude or other depression. I would like to believe, on the contrary, that part of the effects of moderate doses (0,05 to 0,10 g) of coca is maintained more than 24 hours. I observed, at least on myself, the same day as the coca intake, a state that differed favorably from my usual state and it is thus that I explain myself best, by adding up all these side effects, the possibility of this durable strengthening often mentioned.

Observations reported later indicate that moderate and prolonged use of cocaine is unlikely to cause any disturbance in the body. Von Anrep administered moderate doses of coca to animals for 30 days without noting any detrimental effect on body functions. I have experienced this in my own home and in the homes of other knowledgeable observers, and it seems to me to be worth noting: whether it is the first or the umpteenth time that coca is taken, there is no desire to continue taking it, but rather a certain unmotivated disgust with the remedy arises. Perhaps this circumstance has contributed to the fact that coca, in spite of some warm recommendations, has not succeeded in really finding its place as a consumer product.

Mantegazza tested the effects of high doses of coca on himself. He was plunged into a deep joy of life with a tendency to total immobility, itself interrupted from time to time by a very violent need to move. The analogy with the results of von Anrep's animal experiments is obvious. By further increasing the dose, he maintained himself in a "sopor beatus" with an excessive pulse rate and a moderate increase in body temperature. He had difficulty in speaking, his handwriting was uncertain, and he finally had the brightest and richest hallucinations, first of frightening content for a short time, then of constant cheerfulness. This cocaine inebriation did not leave behind any depression or signs of intoxication overcome. Moreno y Maïz also observed a violent need to move after high doses of coca. No disorder of consciousness appeared in Mantegazza, even after the consumption of 18 drachmas of coca leaves; a pharmacist who had taken 1.5 g of cocaine to poison himself[57] had all the symptoms of a gastroenteritis without disorder of consciousness.

VI. The therapeutic use of coca

A plant whose consumption manifested such effects, considered miraculous where it was a local product, could not fail to be used also against the most diverse disorders and diseases of the organism. Thus, the first Europeans who paid attention to this treasure of the indigenous population recommended coca without reservation. Mantegazza, relying on his long experience as a physician, later established a series of therapeutic indications for coca, some of which soon found the approval of other physicians. In what follows I have tried to gather the recommendations in favor of coca reported in the different publications, distinguishing those based on successes with patients, from those derived from considerations concerning the physiological action of coca. In general, the latter have been predominant. It seems that in North America, coca preparations are currently widely used

---

57. Ploss, *Zeitschrift für Chirurgie (Journal of Surgery)*, 1863.

and recognized, while in Europe, the majority of doctors do not even know the name. The poor results that were reported very soon after the introduction of coca in Europe, the dubious quality, the scarcity and the high price of the preparations explain this injustice of which coca is a victim in Europe, an injustice that is, in my opinion, completely undeserved. Among the indications that can be gathered in favor of coca consumption, some are totally guaranteed, others deserve at least a verification free of prejudice. Merck's cocaine and its salts are, as has been proven, preparations whose effect, in totality or for the most part, is due to the coca leaves.

1) Coca as a stimulant

The main use of coca will remain that which the Indians have made of it for centuries: each time it is a question of increasing the physical capacities of the body for a given time and of maintaining them for new solicitations, particularly when the external conditions prevent a rest and an absorption of food corresponding to this surplus of work. For example, in times of war, travel, mountain climbing, expeditions, etc., moments when alcohol is also recognized by all. Coca is a much more powerful and harmless stimulant than alcohol and the only obstacle to its widespread use today is its high price. Based on the effect of coca on the natives of South America, the old author Pedro Crespo (Lima, 1793) already recommended the introduction of coca in the European Navy, as well as Neudörfer (1870), Clemens (1867) and Sergeant Major E. Charles[58] in the European Army, and the experiences

---

58. *Philadelphia Medical and Surgical Reporter*, 1883.

of Aschenbrandt should not fail to draw the attention of the military leadership to coca. For cocaine used as a stimulant, it will be best administered in small effective doses (0.05 to 0.10 g), repeated until the effects of the doses blend together. There seems to be no accumulation of cocaine in the body; the total absence of depressive states after the action of coca has already been pointed out.

It is not possible today to determine with any certainty what can be expected from coca for the increase of intellectual capacities. I had the impression that a prolonged consumption of coca could bring a durable improvement where the blocking was only due to physical causes and fatigue. Obviously, the momentary effect of a dose of coca cannot be compared with an injection of morphine, and therefore there will be no need to fear a general disorder of the body comparable to that caused by chronic consumption of morphine.

For many doctors, cocaine seemed destined to fill a gap in the range of drugs used in psychiatry, which has, as we know, enough means to diminish too much excitation of the nervous centers, but which knows no means to increase their reduced activity. Consequently, coca is recommended against the most diverse states of psychic weakness; against hysteria, hypochondria, melancholic inhibition, stupor, etc. There are even some success stories. The Jesuit Antonio Julian (Lima, 1787) tells that a learned missionary was relieved of a serious hypochondria; Mantegazza affirms that the coca is almost always effective in these cases of functional disorders that we designate today with the name of *neurasthenia*; for Fliessburg, the coca returned excellent services in cases of "nervous prostration"; according to Caldwell[59], it is an excellent tonic in case of hysteria.

E. Morselli and G. Buccola[60] conducted experiments by systematically administering cocaine for several months to melancholic patients. These doses of 0.0025 to 0.10 g of a cocaine prepared by Trommsdorf were administered by subcutaneous injection. After one to two months, they observed a slight improvement in their patients, in that they became more cheerful, ate and enjoyed regular digestion[61].

On the whole, the administration of coca in states of nervous and psychic weakness requires further research which will probably lead to a partly favorable result. During organic modifications and inflammatory states of the nervous system, coca is, according to Mantegazza, useless or even dangerous.

2) Coca and digestive disorders of the stomach

This is the oldest and most justified use of coca, and at the same time the one we understand most easily. According to the concordant indications of the oldest as well as the youngest authors (Julian, Martius, Unanué, Mantegazza, Bingel[62], Scrivener[63], Frankl among others), coca, in its most diverse preparations, eliminates the dyspeptic pains, the annoyance

---

59. "Review of some of our later remedies," *Detroit Therapeutic Gazette*, Dec. 1880.
60. "Ricerche sperimentali sull'azione fisiologica e terapeutica della Cocaina", *Rendiconti del R. Ist. Lombardo*, XIV, 1882.
61. Their indications concerning the physiological effects of cocaine agree with those of Mantegazza. Immediately after an injection of cocaine, the effects observed are: dilation of the pupils, increase of the temperature of one or two degrees, acceleration of the pulse and breathing. No cases of seizures.
62. *Pharmakologisch-therapeutisches Handbuch*, Erlangen, 1862.
63. *Loc. cit.*

and the weakness which are inherent to it, and it leads successfully, in case of prolonged consumption, to a lasting cure. I myself have made a series of observations of this kind.

Just as Mantegazza[64] and Frankl[65] have experienced on themselves, I have painful discomforts after heavy meals - feeling of heaviness and satiety in the stomach, discomfort and unpleasantness at work - and I have seen them disappear thanks to small doses of cocaine (0.025 to 0.05 g) accompanied by dismissals. I have, on numerous occasions, provided some colleagues with the same relief, and twice observed how, after gastric excesses, nausea quickly disappeared thanks to cocaine and gave way to a normal appetite and a subjective feeling of well-being. I also learned to avoid stomach aches by adding a small amount of cocaine to the sodium salicylate I was taking.

My dear colleague, Professor Josef Pollak, has made available to me the following observation of a luminous effect of coca, which shows that cocaine not only suppresses subjective stomach discomforts, but also severe reflexes, in such a way that cocaine can be attributed a powerful effectiveness on the mucous membrane and musculature of this organ.

"A robust man of 42 years of age, perfectly known to the doctor, is compelled to adhere strictly to a certain diet and certain meal times, because he never escapes the setbacks below. He is particularly sensitive when he travels and when

---

64. The detailed stories of the patients of Mantegazza seem to me to be quite plausible.
65. "Mitteilung über Coca von Dr. Josef Frankl" (Communication on coca by Dr. Josef Frankl), spa doctor in Marienbad, *Zeitschrift der K. Gesellschaft der Ärzte*, 1860.

he is under the influence of mood swings. These attacks occur very regularly. They begin in the evening with a feeling of discomfort in the epigastrium. Then appear violent headaches accompanied by an important depression and apathy, at the same time as a reddening of the face, tears in the eyes, beating in the carotids. He spends the night without sleeping; towards the morning, he has several hours of painful vomiting; towards noon, appeasement, by eating a few spoonfuls of soup, the feeling "that a heavy lump which would have weighed for a long time on the stomach would go away at last", then rancid returns, until the normal state returns in the evening. The patient is unable to work all day and must stay in bed.

On June 10 at 8 o'clock in the evening appear the usual symptoms of an attack; at 10 o'clock, while the headaches are already violent, the patient receives 0,075 g of *cocain. muriat.* Shortly afterwards, he has a sensation of hot discharge which still seems to him "too insufficient". At 10:30 am, he receives again 0,075 g of cocaine; the dismissals are amplified; the patient feels lighter, is able to write a long letter. He claims to feel intense movements in the stomach, at midnight; he is in a normal state except for slight headaches, he is even cheerful, walks for an hour, does not manage to fall asleep before 3 a.m., which does not seem painful to him, wakes up the next morning in good health, ready to work and with a good appetite."

The effect of cocaine on the stomach is twofold, as Mantegazza also assumes: stimulation of the movements and decrease of the sensitivity of the stomach. This last point is not only made probable by the subjective sensations following a coca intake, but also by the analogous effect of cocaine on other mucous membranes. Mantegazza claims to have obtained fantastic results in cases of gastralgia and enteralgia, in all painful and convulsive affections of the stomach and intestines, which he explains only by the anesthetic property of coca. In this direction, I cannot confirm the experiences of Mantegazza. I saw the sensitivity of the stomach to pressure decrease after taking coca only once, during a catarrh of the stomach and intestines. The other times I have seen myself, and I have also heard from other doctors, that patients who were diagnosed with ulcers or injuries of the stomach complained of increased pain after taking coca, a fact that can be explained by the increased movements of the stomach.

I therefore affirm that the consumption of coca is quite indicated in cases of atonic weakness of the digestion and for what is called nervous disorders of the stomach. In these conditions, one should not only obtain a relief of the symptoms, but also a lasting improvement.

3) Coca in cases of cachexia

Prolonged consumption of coca is also strongly recommended and has apparently also been successfully tested in all diseases that are accompanied by tissue degeneration: severe anemia, phthisis, long-lasting feverish diseases, etc., and also during convalescence from such diseases. With the consumption of coca, Mc Bean[66] has observed an improvement in constant progression in cases of typhoid fevers. In the cases of phthisis, it is supposed to limit the fever and to attenuate the perspiration. Peckham[67] speaks about a proven case of

---

66. Erythroxylon Coca in the treatment of typhus and typhoid fevers, and also of other febrile diseases, *British Medical Journal*, vol. I, 1877.
67. *Detroit Therapeutic Gazette*, July 1880.

phthisis which improved in a spectacular way after 7 months of consumption of *fluid extract of coca*. Hole[68] cites another rather serious case where a chronic lack of appetite had led to severe weight loss and exhaustion, and yet coca consumption had brought back health. R. Bartholow[69] observed in general for phthisis and for other "processes of degeneration" advantageous effects of coca. Mantegazza as well as many other authors attribute to coca, in the course of therapy, the same invaluable effectiveness consisting, in the cases of cachexia, to limit the degeneration of the body and to increase its forces.

One can try to relate these successes partly to the certainly favorable effect of coca on the digestion of the stomach. But it should be kept in mind that a good part of the authors consider coca as a "saving medium", they are indeed of the opinion that an organism which has absorbed an extremely small amount of cocaine will be able to find a greater amount of energy convertible into work than without coca[70]. During constant work, the organism on cocaine should sustain itself even with lower metabolism, so even with lower food intake.

This assumption was obviously made to clarify von Voit's remark[71] about the unexplained effects of coca on the Indians. Nor does it necessarily contradict the law of conservation of energy. Indeed, in the course of work compensated by food or tissue components, a certain loss occurs - either in the use of the assimilated substances or in the transformation of

---

68. "Coca Erythroxylon in exhaustion," *Detroit Therapeutic Gazette*, Oct. 1880.
69. *Detroit Therapeutic Gazette*, Sept. 1880.
70. Marvaud, *Les Aliments d'épargne*, Paris, 1874.
71. "Physiology of the allgemeinen Stoffwechsels" (Physiology of general metabolism), 1881, *Hermann's Handbuch*, VI, 1.

the accumulated energy into work - which could perhaps be reduced by taking appropriate measures. However, this has not been proven. Experiments designed to determine the amount of urine eliminated with and without coca have not yielded consistent results, but neither have they always been carried out under the conditions under which they could have been conclusive. Moreover, these experiments seem to have been carried out under the assumption that the quantity of urine eliminated - unchanged as we know it to be by the work - allows to measure the general metabolism. Christison thus observed on himself a slight decrease in the solid components of the urine during walks undertaken with coca. Lippmann, Demarle, Marvaud and recently Mason[72] also conclude from their experiments that the absorption of coca decreases the quantity of eliminated urine. Gazeau[73] on the other hand found an increase of 11% to 24% in the elimination of urine under the effect of coca and he explains the deprivation of food and the work capacity that its consumption allows by a better availability of substances accumulated in the body. The elimination of carbonic acid has not been the subject of experiments.

Voit showed that coffee, which is also considered a sparing food, had no influence on albumin uptake in the body. The idea that coca is a sparing food was shaken in experiments in which animals were starved with and without cocaine and determined what was the weight loss, as well as the resistance time to starvation. Such experiments were carried out by Claude Bernard, Moréno y Maïz, Demarle, Gazeau and von

---

72. Erythroxylon Coca, its physiological effect and especially its effect on the excretion of urea by the kidneys, *Boston Medical and Surgical Journal*, 1882.
73. *Comptes-rendus de l'Académie des sciences*, II, 1870.

Anrep. They gave the following results: animals on cocaine succumbed to starvation as quickly, perhaps even more quickly than animals not on cocaine. The historical example reported by Unanué concerning a famine in the city of La Paz, where the inhabitants who had coca escaped death, appears however to contradict these results. We can refer here to the fact that in human beings, the nervous system exerts an unmistakable as well as obscure influence on the feeding of the tissues; psychic disorders can make a healthy man lose weight.

The therapeutic indications from which we started do not seem to be to reject at once; the excitation of the nervous centers by the cocaine can exert a favorable influence on the feeding of the body in case of degeneration, even if this influence does not consist a priori in a slowing down of the metabolism.

It should be added here that coca has also been enthusiastically recommended in the case of syphilis. R. W. Taylor[74] affirms that with cocaine, mercury is better tolerated and the cachexia caused by it disappears, and J. Collan[75] recommends it as the best remedy for mercurial stomatitis and adds that Pagvalin always prescribes it in addition to the mercury preparations.

4) Coca in the detoxification of morphine addicts and alcoholics

In recent years it has been observed in America that coca preparations have the power to restrain the morphine cravings of morphine addicts and to alleviate the severe symptoms of collapse which occur during detoxification. According to the

74. Pathology and Treatment in veneral diseases, *Detroit Therapeutic Gazette*, February 1884.
75. *Loc. cit.*

information I have mainly taken from the *Detroit Therapeutic Gazette*, it was W. H. Bentley who reported in May 1878 that a morphine addict had replaced the alkaloid to which he was accustomed with coca. Two years later, Palmer seems to have awakened general attention thanks to an article in the *Louisville Medical News* concerning this treatment of morphinism, for "erythroxylon coca in the opium habit" constituted for the next two years a permanent feature in the articles of the *Therapeutic Gazette*. From then on, mentions of successful detoxification cures are rarer; whether this is due to the implementation or abandonment of this treatment, I could not say. The small advertisements made by traders in the last issues of American newspapers lead me to favor the first hypothesis.

About 16 papers report successful detoxifications and only one mentions the abandonment of coca by a morphine addict, with the doctor adding that he wonders what these numerous recommendations of coca mean in the case of morphine addiction. Not all success stories are equally persuasive; some involve very large doses of opium or morphine and an addiction that has lasted for years. There is little mention of recidivists since most cases are described very soon after recovery. The symptoms encountered during abstinence are not always described in detail. Of particular importance are the reports that patients discontinued the coca preparation after a few weeks without feeling the need for morphine again[76]. It is repeatedly emphasized that morphine-induced cachexia recedes in favor of a flourishing good health that renders

---

76. J. Brenton, *T. G.*, March 1881. - G. H. Gray from *The Medical Brief*, *T. G.*, June 1881. - H. Leforger, Dec. 1872.

patients unrecognizable[77]. As regards the mode of detoxification, in the majority of cases, the gradual decrease in the usual dose was proportional to the increase in the dose of coca, but brutal detoxifications were also practiced[78]. For the latter, Palmer prescribes a certain dose of coca, to be taken whenever the craving for morphine returns[79]. The daily consumption of coca gradually decreases until the antidote can be dispensed with completely. From the beginning, accidents during abstinence were few and far between, and they proved to be benign after a few days. Almost all the detoxifications were carried out by the patients themselves, whereas detoxification from morphine without recourse to coca, as practiced in Europe, requires the supervision of the patient in a care institution.

I had the opportunity to observe a brutal detoxification through the consumption of coca in a man who, during a previous detoxification, had been victim of severe symptoms during abstinence. This time, his condition was bearable, in particular he did not feel depression or nausea as long as the effect of the coca was maintained; cold and diarrhea were the only permanent symptoms reminding him of his abstinence. The patient did not need to take the bed and he was able to work. The first few days he consumed 3 dg of *cocaine.* After 10 days, he was able to do without the remedy.

In the case of morphine detoxification, therefore, it is not an exchange in which the morphine addict becomes a *coquero,* but only a temporary consumption of coca. Nor do I believe

---

77. E. C. Huse, *T. G.,* Sept. 1880. - Henderson, *T. G.,* February 1881.
78. R. Taggart, *T. G.,* May 1881. - A. F. Stimmel, *T. G.,* June 1881.
79. *T. G.,* June 1880. The preparation used was mostly the *fluid extract* of Parke, Davis & Co.

"A little cocaine to loosen my tongue"

that the overall fortifying effects of coca put the morphine-weakened organism in a position to overcome detoxification by minimizing its symptoms. Rather, I wish to assume that coca has an effect directly opposite to that of morphine, and I can point to a case I borrow from the observations of Dr. Josef Pollak to confirm this view:

"A 33-year-old woman has been suffering for years from severe menstrual migraines from which only a morphine injection relieves her. Although the woman never takes morphine during periods when she does not have migraines, and does not feel the urge to do so, she nevertheless behaves like a morphine addict during her attacks. A few hours after the injection, she suffered from severe depression, nausea and vomiting, which was stopped by another shot of morphine, which led to further symptoms of intolerance, so that each attack left her bedridden and miserable for three days. She was then given cocaine for the migraine, which proved useless. Morphine injections had to be reintroduced, but when the morphine intolerance symptoms reappeared, they were quickly suppressed with 1 dg of cocaine, so that the patient was able to overcome the attack in a much shorter time and with much less morphine use."

At the same time as it was used against morphinism, coca was prescribed in America against chronic alcoholism, and it is mainly Einem who reported on it[80]. Here too, success was achieved without any doubt. The irresistible urge to drink was reabsorbed or relieved and the dyspeptic pains of the drinker

---

80. W. H. Bentley, *T. G.*, Sept. 1880. - Volum, Jan. 1881. - H. Warner, March 1881. - Stimmel, Apr. and Jul. 1881. -

were improved. Coca was generally more effective in removing the craving for alcohol than the addiction to morphine; Bentley reports a case where the *potator* became a *coquero*. We will limit ourselves to mentioning the unheard-of boom that this "saving food" - we are talking about coca - could take for a national economy if its effectiveness in the detoxification of alcoholics was confirmed.

5) Coca against asthma

Tschudi and Markham[81] tell that while climbing the Andes, they escaped the so-called *mountain sickness*, which consists of a complex of symptoms with dyspnea, heartbeat, dizziness, etc., by chewing coca leaves. - Poizat[82] reports that the asthma attacks of a patient were each time interrupted thanks to coca. I add this prescription of coca because it seems to be physiologically justified. In his animal experiments, von Anrep found a rapid paralysis of certain branches of the vagus nerve, and both altitude-induced asthma and attacks in chronic bronchitis can be analyzed as reflex excitations of the pulmonary branches of the vagus nerve. It should be examined what use coca has been made of in other vagus nerve neuroses.

6) Coca as an aphrodisiac

In South America, the natives who represented their goddess of the love with leaves of coca to the hand did not doubt the exciting effect of the coca on the genital spheres. Mantegazza confirms that the *coqueros* preserve elevated faculties until an

---

81. *Travels in Peru and India,* 1862.
82. "The Erythroxylon Coca in Asthma," *Philadelphia Medical and Surgical Reporter,* 1881.

"A little cocaine to loosen my tongue"

advanced age, he even evokes cases of recovery of the faculties and disappearance of symptoms of functional weakness following the consumption of coca, but he prefers to believe that this effect of the coca does not appear in all the individuals. Marvaud maintains with aplomb that coca has a stimulating effect, other authors recommend coca occasionally during functional weakness and temporary exhaustion, and Bentley reports the recovery of a similar case[83].

Of the people I have given coca to, three have told me of a violent sexual arousal which they unhesitatingly attribute to coca. One young writer who was able to get back to work after a long upset with coca gave up using coca because of this undesirable side effect.

7) Local application of coca

The anaesthetic property of cocaine and its salts on the skin and on the mucous membranes with which it comes into contact in concentrated solution invites its occasional use, especially in case of mucous membrane affections. According to Collin[84], Ch. Fauvel praises cocaine in the treatment of pharyngeal diseases and characterizes it as "the tensor par excellence of the vocal cords"[85]. Many other applications of cocaine based on its anaesthetic property should be found.

---

83. *T. G.*, December 1880.
84. "Of coca and its true therapeutic properties", *The Medical Union*, 1877.
85. In French in the text (N.D.T.).

CONTRIBUTION TO THE KNOWLEDGE OF THE EFFECTS OF COCA (1885)

Having carried out a study on the cocaine derivative *ecgonin* for the Merck company, and not having been able to obtain sufficient elements for a publication, due to the lack of usable results, Freud took this opportunity to continue his research and to write this article, the first edition of which dates from 1885 (*Wiener medizinische Wochenschrift*, vol. 35, January 31, pp. 129-133).

I published a study on coca and its alkaloid[86], cocaine, in the July issue of the *Centralblatt für Therapie* edited by Dr. Heitler, which recommended this long-neglected remedy to the attention of physicians, based on a review of the experiments reported in the literature and those I myself had conducted. I can say that the success of this suggestion was surprisingly rapid and significant. While Dr. L. Königstein

---

86. "Über Coca," *Centralblatt für die gesammte Therapie*, Year II, VII, July (not August, as has been erroneously mentioned many times) 1884.

undertook at my request to test the effectiveness of cocaine on pain and on the limitation of secretions in cases of eye diseases, my colleague in this hospital, Professor Karl Koller, had the bright idea, independently of my own suggestions, to develop total anesthesia and analgesia of the cornea and conjunctiva, the anesthetic property of cocaine on the sensitivity of the mucous membranes having been known for a long time[87]. In addition, the important practical utility of this local anaesthesia was revealed through experiments on animals and surgical operations on human beings. Following Koller's presentation on this subject at this year's Congress of Ophthalmologists in Heidelberg, cocaine was unanimously adopted as a local anesthetic.

As an extension of my study on cocaine, I tried to determine objective symptoms and to observe in detail the miraculous effects of this alkaloid which stimulates mood, bodily and intellectual capacities and endurance. The experience of the diversity of subjective symptoms of the effects of coca in different people also pushed me to this undertaking. While some indicate an even brighter euphoria than I have described about myself, others feel uncomfortable, confused, under the obvious influence of a toxic product. Schroff Sr. also seems to have fallen into the latter category, as he was the first to test the effect of cocaine (1862), and this fortuitous personal disposition is partly responsible for the long sidelining of the alkaloid. I hope, therefore, that a methodical and

---

87. The seventh of the prescriptions I have mentioned for the use of cocaine relates to its local application and ends with the words, "Many other applications of cocaine based on its anesthetic property should be found."

objective observation will reveal a greater uniformity of the effects of cocaine.

In order to define the effects of coca through variations observed on measurable quantities - perhaps in various directions - I chose to observe the motor force of a particular muscle group, as well as the psychic time of reaction. The first experiment is done with the help of a dynamometer, an elastic metal bracelet whose compression moves an arrow along a graduated ruler, which stops as soon as the pressure is released. I had at my disposal two such objects, the first one was heavy and gave significant results because it could be compressed with both hands, but it had the disadvantage of generating a great expenditure of energy and a rapid fatigue, and the other one was a light dynamometer that could be activated with only one hand, built according to the plans of Dr. von Burq. I quickly gained confidence in the results of the dynamometers, the effects of the pressure, especially the maxima, being largely independent of the person arbitrarily chosen to exert that pressure, and the manner in which it is exerted modifying it only slightly and insignificantly. The observation of the psychic reaction time was made with the help of Exner's neuroamoebimeter, which essentially consists of a metallic tongue set to 100 undulations per second, the person who activates it interrupting the vibration as soon as he perceives the sound produced by the release of the tongue. The time that elapses between the perception of the sound and the withdrawal of the tongue is the reaction time, and it is given directly in hundredths of a second by the number of undulations of the tongue. For a more precise description of this small device and the precautions necessary for this kind of experiment, I refer to Exner's text "Experimentelle Untersuchung der einfachsten psychischen Prozesse[88]" (Experimental studies of the simplest psychic processes). Dr. Herzig was kind enough to work with me on these laborious experiments.

These two series of experiments, I carried them out on many occasions, on myself, or by having them carried out. I know that such experiments on oneself present the disadvantage, for the person who carries them out, to pretend to a double objectivity, but I had to proceed thus for reasons independent of my will, and because none of the individuals that I had at my disposal reacted in such a homogeneous way to cocaine. The results of the experiments were confirmed on this point by observations I made on other people, mostly colleagues.

The result of the observations with the dynamometer was that 0,05 to 0,10 g of *cocain. muriat.* increases notably the motor force of the arms, the maximum point being reached at home in 10 to 15 minutes at the same time as the euphoria of the coca and being maintained in a lesser measure during several hours. Here are the details of some experiments:

Experiment of November 9, 1884. Dynamometer for two hands. Pressures are indicated in pounds. To study the influence of fatigue, the pressure was exerted three times in succession for each experiment.

---

88. *Pflüger's Archiv*, VII, Anhang zur genannten Abhandlung (*Pflüger's Archive*, Appendix to the cited study).

Time	Pressures	Maxima	Average	Note
8 a.m.	66 - 65 - 60	66	63,6	on an empty stomach
10 a.m.	67 - 55 - 50	67	57,3	after the morning visit
10:22 a.m.	67 - 63 - 56			
10:30 a.m.	65 - 58 - 67	67	63,6	-
10:33 a.m.	0.10 *cocainum muriaticum*			
10:45 a.m.	82 - 75 - 69	82	75,3	followed by a first vomit
10:55 a.m.	76 - 69 - 64	76	69,6	tired
11:20 a.m.	78 - 71 - 77	78	75,3	euphoria
12:30 p.m.	72 - 66 - 74	74	70,6	before lunch
12:55 p.m.	72 - 73 - 67	77	72,6	-
1:35 p.m.	75 - 66 - 74	75	71,6	after lunch
1:50 p.m.	76 - 71 - 61			
3:35 p.m.	65 - 58 - 62	65	61,6	past euphoria

As can be seen, cocaine caused a considerable increase in motor strength, whether judged by the averages or by the maxima in the upper table, and this was maintained for about 5 hours. My general condition on the day of the experiment was poor and my motor strength low.

Another experiment will show the effect of cocaine with initially higher numbers for motor strength.

Experiment of November 10, 1884. The same dynamometer.

Time	Pressures	Maxima	Average	Note
8 a.m.	60	66	63,6	tired
10 a.m.	73 - 63 - 67	67	57,3	after the visit
10 a.m.	taking an undetermined low dose of cocaine			
10:20 a.m.	76 - 70 - 76	76	74	happier
10:30 a.m.	73 - 70 - 68	73	70,3	-
11:35 a.m.	72 - 72 - 74	74	72,6	-
12:50 p.m.	74 - 73 - 63	74	70	-
2:20 p.m.	70 - 68 - 69	70	69	-
4:00 p.m.	76 - 74 - 75	76	75	normal condition
6:00 p.m.	67 - 64 - 58	67	63	after a hard job
8:30 p.m.	74 - 64 - 67	74	68,3	a little tired
-	0.1 g of *cocainum muriaticum*			
8:43 p.m.	80 - 73 - 74	80	75,6	vomit
8:58 p.m.	79 - 76 - 71	79	75,3	-
9:18 p.m.	77 - 72 - 67	77	72	feeling of lightness

As I continued these experiments for several weeks, two facts struck me: first, that the figures for the motor force of a muscle group during the course of a day showed regular variations, and second, that these same figures reached quite different values on different days. These are points which have little to do with the effects of coca, but which are perhaps interesting enough to merit some remarks.

The following table will show the daily variations of the driving force in my case.

"A little cocaine to loosen my tongue"

Experiment of November 27 and 28, 1884. Pressures in kilograms; Burq's dynamometer; the figures correspond to the maximums with triple pressure of the right hand.

Time	Maxima	Note	Time	Maxima	Note
7:20 a.m.	32	at sunrise	7:20 a.m.	32	at sunrise
9:30 a.m.	35	after the visit, on an empty stomach	7:50 a.m.	34-35	on an empty stomach
		visit, on an empty stomach			
12 p.m.	37+	after working several hours	10 a.m.	37-	after the visit
2:45 p.m.	37-	after a coffee, otherwise on an empty stomach	10:30 a.m.	36-37	after breakfast
4 p.m.	38	after a class	1:40 p.m.	36	after working
5:45 p.m.	37+	after working three hours	2:40 p.m.	36	before a class
6:45 p.m.	38-	-	4 p.m.	36	after a class
7:15 p.m.	35+	tired	5:30 p.m.	36	after the visit
8 p.m.	36,5	calm	8:30 p.m.	37	after a coffee
9:15 p.m.	34	after dinner	10:30 p.m.	35+	after dinner

From all these observations and others it can be deduced that the motor force is weakest in the morning - it only wakes up partially, so to speak -, that it increases rapidly to reach its maximum level during the morning, a level at which it remains throughout the day and that it slowly but steadily decreases in the evening, without reaching the morning minimum. Tiring work, as long as it did not generate too much fatigue, seemed to me to increase motor capacity instead. I could not determine what influence meals or their absence had. It is tempting to relate the daily variations of the motor force to the temperature curve.

Once I had completed these observations, my attention was drawn to a preliminary report by Dr. Max Buch[89] which deals with the daily variations of the motor force. Buch's indications diverge from mine in the following point: after a maximum in the afternoon, he finds a drop to a second lower maximum in the evening, which only then precedes the drop at night. I cannot say whether the small difference between our results is due to the different ways of life or to the fact that Buch was experimenting with a graduated instrument with smaller units (1/4 kg). Buch also mentions an inaugural dissertation by Powarnin which already emphasizes the essential fact, the minimum force in the morning.

I have already mentioned as a second important fact that the driving force reaches different values on different days, so that its variations during the day are at a higher or lower level. So there were days when I started with a minimum of 28 kg and could not reach a maximum of more than 35 kg. The biggest difference between the maximum and the minimum in one day was 6 kg for me, while the biggest difference between these same values on different days was only 4 kg.

It has become quite clear to me that the above-mentioned time-independent variations in motor power express a general state, the subjective manifestation of which as a state

---

89. Über die Tagesschwankungen der Muskelkraft des Menschen (About the daily variations of the motive power of the human being), *Berliner klin. Wochenschr*, no. 28, 1884.

of mind or mood is in part related to motor ability. I am of the opinion that coca does not act directly - for example on the motor nerve substance or on the muscles - but indirectly, by generating a better general state. Two factors support this idea: firstly, the most significant increase in motor strength occurs quickly after taking coca, at a time when the coca-induced euphoria is already present, but when not all the cocaine can be assimilated by the body; secondly, the increase in motor strength is much greater when cocaine acts on a poor state of health and weak motor strength. However, the figures reached afterwards on cocaine still exceed the maximum figures reached in a normal state.

When, in order to define the state of an individual, we take into consideration the value of physical constants measurable in a living being, we of course give priority to values that do not present any significant individual variation, such as temperature. To define the different states of a certain individual, the driving force of an important muscle group is not to be rejected.

Experiments concerning the effects of cocaine on reaction time have yielded a similar, overall less clear result. I observed several times that my reaction time on cocaine was shorter and more uniform than before taking cocaine, but I sometimes had equally advantageous psychic reactions when I found myself in a happy and energetic mood. The variations in reaction time are thus an element of the euphoria generated by coca, to which I also attributed the increase in muscle strength.

Experiment of November 26, 1884

Time	Reaction time	Max	Min	Average	Note
7:10 p.m.	15 ½ - 21 ½ - 19 - 21 - 18 ½ - 24 - 24	24	15 ½	of 7 experiences 20,5	driving force, 36-, tired
	at 7:30 p.m., 0,10 g of *cocainum muriaticum*				
7:38 p.m.	17 - 21 ½ - 16 - 21 - 17 - 16	21 ½	16	of 6 experiences 18	driving force 39+
8:05 p.m.	17 - 17 - 18 - 17	18	17	of 4 experiences 17,2	a little more cocaine
8:15 p.m.	13 ½ - 11 - 16 - 15 - 16 - 12	16	11	of 6 experiences 13,9	euphoria
10:30 p.m.	15 ½ - 14 ½ - 15 - 13 ½ - 17 ½	17 ½	14 ½	of 5 experiences 15,2	well-being that is maintained, driving force 37,5

Experiment of December 4, 1884 in the best state of health without cocaine

Time	Reaction time	Max	Min	Average	Note
8:15 p.m.	13 ½ - 13 - 14 ½ - 13 ½	14 ½	13	of 4 experiences 13,6	driving force 38-39 kg
8:30 p.m.	15 - 14 - 14 - 19 - 15 ½ - 15 ½	19	14	of 6 experiences 15,5	at the time of the reaction, annoying noise
8:45 p.m.	11 ½ - 13 ½ - 14 ½ - 12 ½ - 16 ½				
9 p.m.	12 ½ - 13 - 13 - 15 ½ - 14 - 18 ½	18 ½	12 ½	of 6 experiences 14,2	driving force 38

About the General Action of Cocaine

Before giving this talk in Vienna on March 5, 1885, at the Psychiatric Society (Psychiatrischer Verein), Freud had already given it at the Physiological Club, a less formal gathering of physicians.

Last summer, I devoted myself to the study of the physiological effects and therapeutic use of cocaine. And I offer this presentation today because I feel that some aspects of it may also be of interest to a psychiatric society. I am therefore totally disregarding the use of cocaine in external application which was so successfully introduced by Koller in ophthalmology and which also renders valuable services in other branches of practical medicine. We will only focus on the effects of internally applied cocaine.

With the conquest of the South American countries by the Spaniards, we learned that coca leaves served as a consumer product for the natives and that they had, according to the most reliable reporters, extraordinary working capacities. It is therefore understandable that great hopes were raised in Europe when the Novara expedition brought back a certain quantity of coca leaves and a student of Wöhler in Göttingen, Niemann, prepared a new alkaloid, cocaine, from them. Since then, many experiments have been carried out with this substance, as with the leaves themselves, in order to achieve a result similar to that of coca on the Indians, but these efforts generally caused great disappointment and a tendency to doubt the veracity of the reports coming from the coca countries. I will not discuss the probable reasons for this failure here; however, at this time - between 60 and 70 years ago - there are also some accounts of the increased work capacity that cocaine generates. In the winter of 1883, Dr. von Aschenbrandt reported that Bavarian soldiers in a state of extreme fatigue due to exhaustion, heat, etc., felt rested after receiving very small amounts of *cocaine. muriat.* My merit consists perhaps only in the fact that I believed in this communication. It was an opportunity for me to study the effects of coca on myself, as well as on other people.

I can describe the effects of cocaine when used internally as follows: if one takes an effective dose (0.05 to 0.10 g) in an excellent state of health and with no particular effort on one's part, the effects experienced will go almost unnoticed. It will be different, however, if this dose of cocaine hydrochloride is taken during a deterioration of the general state due to fatigue or hunger. It takes only 10 to 20 minutes to feel at the height of one's intellectual and physical alertness, one feels a euphoria which differs from that experienced after alcohol consumption only by the absence of pathological alteration. As amazing as this effect of cocaine absorption is, the absence of characteristics differentiating this state from the normal euphoria of a healthy person contributes to underestimate it. As soon as one has forgotten the contrast between the present state and the state before taking cocaine, it is difficult to believe that one is under the effect of an external agent, and yet, for 4 to 5 hours, one is in a completely different state. As long as the effect of cocaine is maintained, one is able to perform intellectual and physical work with great endurance, and the usual imperative to rest, eat and sleep is swept away. In the first few hours after taking cocaine, it is impossible to fall asleep. After a while, this effect of the alkaloid gradually disappears without causing a depressive state.

In my study "Über Coca" (published by Heitler in the *Centralblatt für die gesammte Therapie*, July 1884; reprinted in Moritz-Perles, 1885), I gave many examples, mainly observed on colleagues who had taken cocaine at my request, of disappearance of justified sensations of fatigue and hunger, etc. Since then, I have had many similar experiences. For example, in a writer who had previously been unable to produce any literary work for weeks and who, after 0.1 g of *cocaine, was* able to work for 14 hours without interruption. But it could not escape me that individual disposition plays an important role in the action of cocaine, perhaps a more important role than for other alkaloids. The subjective symptoms due to taking cocaine are different for each person, there are few who show, like me, pure euphoria without pathological alterations. With the same amount of cocaine, others already feel the symptoms of a slight intoxication, a need to move and a great loquacity; in others still, the subjective symptoms of the action of cocaine

About the general action of cocaine

are completely absent. The increase of the working capacities, on the other hand, proved to be a constant symptom of the action of cocaine and I tried to give an objective image of it, especially thanks to the variation of values easy to observe in living beings and referring to physical and psychic capacities. For this purpose, I chose to observe the force used during a particular action with a dynamometer and to determine the psychic reaction time with the Exner neuroamoebimeter. A dynamometer is, as we know, an elastic metal bracelet. When compressed, it moves an arrow along a graduated arc on which the force required to apply pressure can be read in pounds or kilos. Such an instrument is usable when it is correctly graduated, when it does not require too much effort to manipulate, and when, in exerting this pressure, we perform an action similar to that which is frequently exerted in our daily lives with our limbs, a form of movement which is therefore in some way already inscribed in our nervous system. With my arm outstretched, I applied pressure with one or both hands and I was soon convinced that it is very easy to obtain constant figures or constant variations with this instrument. The result of my observations was very striking. 0.4 g of *cocaine. muriat.* increases the strength of one hand from 2 to 3 kg, that of both hands from 3 to 4 kg, this effect appearing after a few minutes, about the same time as the euphoria, then gradually receding in the same time. During these dynamometric measurements, I was able to confirm the fact established by Mr. Buch that muscle strength and temperature undergo a regular daily variation. One's motor skills are at a minimum in the morning when one wakes up; they increase rapidly in the morning, reach a maximum in the afternoon and slowly decrease in the evening. The difference between maximum and minimum for me was 4 kg.

I found a second variation in muscle strength independent of the time of day: on some days one starts from a lower minimum and reaches a lower maximum, so that the daily variation takes place at a lower level. I have never been able to establish a correlation between this decrease in muscle strength and a more morose general state, and I have been inclined to think that cocaine does not act on the motor apparatus, but increases the general disposition to work. It is also necessary to take into consideration the fact that the action of cocaine becomes more striking when it is observed with a motor force of a lower value. It is less so when one is in a perfect state of health and at the maximum of his muscular capacities. The determination of the psychic reaction time has led to the same result as the dynamometric examinations. The psychic reaction time is of course the time between the perception of a sensation and the appearance of a predetermined motor reaction. This time is given in hundredths of a second by Exner's small device thanks to the number of vibrations that a tongue could register on a tray full of soot, until it was interrupted by the reaction of the person in question. The sound produced when the vibrating tab is released serves as the stimulus for the reaction. It turned out that previously uneven and prolonged reaction times were shortened and evened out in my case by the cocaine. On the other hand, I had other times equally advantageous reactions when I did the experiments in the best state of health without cocaine. Here again, the relationship between the effect of cocaine and the euphoria it caused was obvious.

I come now to the two points which are of direct psychiatric interest. Psychiatry has many means of decreasing nervous activity in cases of overexcitation, but it has few means of increasing the faculties of a weakened nervous system. One is tempted, for this reason, to consider the use of the effects of cocaine described above in diseases which we explain as being states of weakness and depression of the nervous system without organic lesions. Since it has been known, cocaine has indeed been used against hysteria, hypochondria, etc., and there is no lack of reports of the cure thus obtained. Only Morselli and Buccola have used cocaine on a larger scale and in a more systematic way in melancholic patients, and they report having obtained slight improvements. On the whole, it must be said that the usefulness of cocaine in psychiatric practice is yet to be proven and will seem to merit careful consideration as soon as this currently unaffordable drug becomes cheaper.

One can evoke in a more assured way another interest of cocaine for the psychiatrist. It is in America that the first experiments were made showing the capacity of cocaine to reduce the worrying symptoms occurring during abstinence in detoxification cures with morphine addicts, and showing its faculty to relieve the need for morphine. The *Detroit Therapeutic Gazette* has published in the last few years a whole series of reports concerning morphine and opium detoxification cures which have been done with the help of cocaine. It should be noted, for example, that patients did not need constant medical supervision during detoxification since they were instructed to take an effective dose of cocaine as often as the need for morphine arose. I myself had the opportunity to observe a case of detoxification - a very brutal one - on cocaine and I could see that the person who had shown the most severe symptoms of collapse during a previous detox was now able to work and stay on his feet, and that only chills, diarrhea and an occasional need for morphine reminded him of his abstinence. The daily dose of cocaine was about 0.40 g and abstinence was overcome in about 20 days. There were no signs of coca addiction; on the contrary, the growing disgust with cocaine use was evident. On the basis of all the experiences I have gathered concerning the action of cocaine, I would advise without hesitation, during similar detoxification cures, to give cocaine in subcutaneous injections in doses of 0.03 to 0.05 g and to increase the doses without fear. I have also observed that cocaine quickly disappeared the symptoms of intolerance that appeared after a larger dose of morphine, as if it had a specific antidote effect against morphine. Recently, in Pankow (see *Neurologisches Centralblatt* of January 1, 1885), Richter confirmed the results of his experiments concerning the value of cocaine in morphine addicts. I am well aware that cocaine has not seemed to be very useful in some detoxification cures, and I expect that the diversity of individual reactions works against the alkaloid. Finally, I think I should add that American physicians will be able to report on the cures or the favorable action of cocaine in curing alcoholism.

Notes on Cocaine Addiction and Cocainephobia

In connection with a presentation by W. A. Hammonds

Publications on the side effects and dangers of cocaine had multiplied since 1885. Neurologists were also interested in the debate.

In 1887, many articles were published on the use of cocaine. Among them, Freud's was the only one to advocate cocaine in cases of detoxification from morphine, and the only one to be concerned with possible addiction. This theme was widely debated. However, Freud did not enter into these debates, he gave the opinion of an American expert who agreed with him, William A. Hammond, retired surgeon general of the American army and professor in New York, internationally recognized in the field of nervous and mental diseases. He had published a paper on addiction in November 1886.

This latest study by Freud on cocaine is therefore not a new contribution, but rather a defense of the position he had previously taken, based on the findings of other researchers.

Karl Koller's brilliant use of the anaesthetic properties of cocaine to treat the sick and to accelerate medical progress made us forget for a while that this new drug had a notable role in the therapy of internal and nervous diseases. One of these uses of cocaine mentioned in my work "Über Coca" published in July 1884 in the *Centralblatt für Therapie* did get the general attention of physicians. It was about the usefulness of cocaine to combat the craving for morphine and the disturbing symptoms of collapse appearing in morphine addicts undergoing detoxification. I had pointed out these properties of cocaine by referring to American reports (in the *Detroit Therapeutic Gazette*) and at the same time reported on the surprisingly favorable course of the first morphine detoxification undertaken on the continent with cocaine. (It may not be superfluous to mention that this was not an experiment on myself, but an opinion I had given to someone else)

During the Copenhagen congress, Professor H. Obersteiner took advantage of this same remark to inform the assembled doctors of the effectiveness of cocaine in cases of morphine detoxification. But he made little impression; it was not until the circular of the chemical factory E. Merck in Darmstadt and a dithyrambic article by Wallé in the *Deutsche Medizinalzeitung* (No. 3, 1885) that the new use of cocaine became known to all doctors - and unfortunately also to morphine addicts.

There followed an energetic opposition from Erlenmeyer (in the *Centralblatt*, 1885), an author who denied any usefulness of cocaine in morphine detoxification, on the basis of a series of experiments which high figures made impressive. He also considered it a dangerous remedy because of its action on vascular innervation. However, Erlenmeyer's results were based on a serious error that was immediately discovered by Obersteiner, Smidt and Rank... Instead of giving effective doses (of several decigrams) orally, as I had proposed, Erlenmeyer had given minimal amounts by subcutaneous injections, and had obtained a short-lived toxic effect from a dose that was ineffective over time. The authors who opposed his conclusions provided full confirmation of my own indications.

The value of cocaine for morphine addicts was however obscured for other reasons. The patients themselves seized the remedy to subject it to the same abuses they were accustomed to with morphine; cocaine was to replace morphine for them and it must have proved insufficient since most morphine addicts quickly reached the enormous dose of 1 g per day by subcutaneous injection. It turned out that such a use of cocaine makes it much more dangerous for health than morphine. The slow slump is replaced by a rapid physical and moral deterioration, hallucinatory states of excitement comparable to *delirium tremens*, a chronic persecution delusion which manifests itself characteristically, according to our experiments, by hallucinatory sensations of small animals under the skin, and the need for cocaine replaces the need for morphine - these were the sad results of the experiment of exorcising the devil by Beelzebub. Many morphine addicts who still had a certain social position only turned to cocaine. Erlenmeyer, who was able to continue to express his disapproval of the new alkaloid with greater success after his first publications on "cocaine addiction", spoke of a "third scourge" of mankind, which was even more dreadful than the first two (alcohol and morphine).

The first information from ophthalmologists and ear, nose and throat specialists about the toxic effects of cocaine use came at about the same time, so that cocaine became known as an extremely dangerous remedy whose prolonged use causes "dependence", a "morphine-like state". I find just such a warning in the latest publication on cocaine (by O. Chiari, this *Wochenschrift* no. 8).

I think we have gone too far. I cannot suppress a remark that might take the sting out of cocaine, which Erlenmeyer pathetically called the third scourge of mankind. *All reports of cocaine addiction and the deterioration it causes refer to morphine addicts*, people who had already succumbed to this demon, and whose weakened will and need for narcotics would and did misuse any stimulant available to them. *Cocaine has not claimed any other victims, any victims of its own.* I have experienced prolonged use of cocaine on multiple occasions in people who were not morphine addicts, and I have also taken the drug for months without feeling or observing anything close to morphinism or a desire to continue cocaine use. On the contrary, a disgust with the drug occurred more often than I wanted it to and caused an adjustment in its dosage. My experiences concerning the usefulness of cocaine in certain states of nervousness and the absence of possible dependence overlap so perfectly on this subject with the communications recently made by a famous foreign authority, W. Hammond, that I prefer to pass on Hammond's assertions rather than repeat what I said in my work "Über Coca" (*Centralblatt für Therapie*, 1884) and in a later article ("Beitrag zur Kenntnis der Cocawirkung," Contribution to the Knowledge of the Effects of Coca, *Wr.*

Med. Wochenschrift, No. 5, 1885). I only want to add a few remarks beforehand about the severe cocaine intoxications observed by ophthalmologists and laryngologists.

Some of these are merely the collapsed states inherent in the aftermath of any operation, especially on sensitive parts of the body, and cannot be attributed to the alkaloid often used in minimal quantities. However, another series of these observations undoubtedly has all the characteristics of cocaine intoxication, the symptoms that appeared being quite similar to those that can be generated experimentally by the absorption of too large a dose of cocaine: stupor, dizziness, increased pulse rate, altered breathing, lack of appetite, insomnia, and sometimes even delirium and muscle weakness. Such states provoked without any doubt by cocaine occurred sometimes after resorption of the remedy by the mucous membranes of the head, other times, and it is the most frequent case, after a subcutaneous injection. It should be noted that these are rare events in proportion to the frequency of cocaine use in the last two years. They have not endangered any lives, most doctors are rightly of the opinion that the possible toxic effects of cocaine do not prevent the use of the remedy to achieve serious operative purposes. It is important to note that such intoxications also occur at very small doses, so the sensitivity of some individuals to cocaine, given the lack of reaction after larger doses in others, has been considered precisely as an idiosyncrasy. I now believe that this unpredictability of cocaine - one does not know when a toxic effect will occur - is very closely related to another unpredictable factor that I am forced to blame on the alkaloid: one does not really know when and in whom cocaine will take effect. (I am, of course, disregarding its anaesthetic effect.) The following context might help us to understand this particularity: cocaine has a quite obvious effect on vascular innervation. When used locally, it produces, as can be seen on any eye that has been treated with cocaine, a vasoconstriction, i.e. an ischemia of the tissues. According to B. Fränkel (discussion on November 4, 1885 at the Berlin Society of Physicians), cocaine generates a vasodilatation on the tongue of curarized frogs, a vasoconstriction appears only from a dilution of 1/20000. According to Erlenmeyer, injected in doses of 0.005 g, cocaine has a paralyzing effect on the vasomotor centers and lowers blood pressure; according to Litten (discussion, etc.), it is particularly tonic, increasing blood pressure. I could add a whole series of apparently contradictory indications from different researchers whose only concordant conclusion is that cocaine has an effect on the blood vessels which varies according to the concentration, the mode of administration, as well as the individual sensitivity. I note here that the description of severe cocaine intoxication sometimes indicates vasoconstriction, sometimes vascular paralysis. It seems to me, therefore, that the variable on which the heterogeneity of the effects of cocaine is based is the uniqueness of each moment and the instability of the innervation of the vessels. That the sensitivity of the vasomotor nerves (or centers) in different people is very diverse and varies within an individual seems to me to be beyond doubt. The instability of the innervation of the cerebral vessels is probably one of the principal symptoms of nervousness. Just think of the different effects of sending a galvanic current to the back, depending on whether it is done in a healthy person or in a nervous person of this or that constitution. In the same way, if the general effect of cocaine is conditioned by the cerebral circulation, it will sometimes - with a stable vascular tone - have no effect, and will sometimes have a toxic effect accompanied by rapid variations; in other cases, it will have a favorable, tonifying or hyper-dynamizing effect. I therefore assume that *the reason for the heterogeneity of the effects of cocaine lies in the diversity of individual sensitivity and the diversity of the state of the vasomotor nerves on which cocaine has an effect.*

As the reason for this sensitivity is generally unknown, and as little consideration has been given to this factor due to individual disposition, I consider it advisable to refrain, if possible, from using cocaine by subcutaneous injection in the treatment of internal and nervous diseases.

W. Hammond spoke as follows at a meeting of the Neurological Society of New York on November 2, 1886[90]:

He used a cocaine wine prepared according to his directions (2 grains of hydrochloric salt to a pint of wine) and made numerous experiments on himself and others. This coca preparation had excellent results in cases of so-called *spinal irritation*, results that he could not attribute to wine alone. It also served as a tonic and a remedy for fatigue; he himself used to take a glass of wine after a tiring day and found himself invigorated every time, without any depression following.

He would have also used the preparation in some cases of dyspepsia accompanied by a great irritability of the stomach, and observed a particularly calming effect. He gave it in doses of two to three teaspoons every 15 to 20 minutes until the sixth

---

90. Summarized remarks.

Notes on cocaine addiction and cocainephobia

dose. Most of the time, the first teaspoonful was given back, but the following ones were kept longer, until the vomiting stopped. Cases of stomach irritability probably related to spinal irritation (neurasthenia) were relieved within a few hours by this treatment.

Dr. Hammond then briefly discussed the physiological effects of coca and pointed out that the first authors to report on its use by indigenous people in South America greatly exaggerated the harm done. Their accounts were constantly reused later without further indication of the source and thus maintained the prevailing prejudice today. In order to verify the validity of the recent newspaper reports about the risky effects of cocaine, he repeatedly injected himself with cocaine and described in detail the slightly toxic effect. But he did not fall victim to any addiction, he was able to give up this remedy at will. Regarding the alleged addiction to cocaine, he informed me that he had given the remedy to a lady suffering from Graves' disease in doses of 1 to 5 grains for three months. She also stopped the treatment without any trouble. In this way he managed to overcome a dependence on morphine and the patient did not become dependent on it. In all these patients, as in himself, cocaine generated an extraordinary increase in cardiac activity, an increase in blood pressure and temperature, as well as profuse sweating and insomnia.

In three cases of melancholy in women who no longer spoke, he succeeded in getting the patients to speak thanks to injections of cocaine, which was sometimes of decisive use.

Dr. Hammond puts cocaine addiction on the same level as coffee or tea addiction, but he differentiates it completely from morphine addiction. He does not believe that there is a single documented case of cocaine addiction (except in morphine addicts), and therefore that patients are not able to give up the drug at will. If someone were to take cocaine for a long time, the damage would probably be to the heart rather than to other organs.

Table of Contents

BEST SELLERS MAX MILO EDITIONS

Hitler's banker, Jean-François Bouchard

Confessions of a forger, Éric Piedoie Le Tiec

The Koran and the flesh, Ludovic-Mohamed Zahed

Governing by fake news, Jacques Baud

Governing by chaos, Collectif

A political history of food, Paul Ariès

Mad in U.S.A.: The ravages of the "American model",
Michel Desmurget

Mondial soccer club geopolitics, Kévin Veyssière

Putin: Game master?, Jacques Braud

Treatise on the three impostors: Moses, Jesus, Muhammad,
The Spirit of Spinoza

TV Lobotomy, Michel Desmurget